Murat Halstead, Florus Beardsley Plimpton, Cordelia A. (Bushnell) Plimpton

Poems of Florus B. Plimpton

Murat Halstead, Florus Beardsley Plimpton, Cordelia A. (Bushnell) Plimpton

Poems of Florus B. Plimpton

ISBN/EAN: 9783744709743

Printed in Europe, USA, Canada, Australia, Japan

Cover: Foto ©Thomas Meinert / pixelio.de

More available books at **www.hansebooks.com**

POEMS

OF

FLORUS B. PLIMPTON

ILLUSTRATED.

CINCINNATI:
MRS. F. B. PLIMPTON.
1886.

PRESS OF
McDONALD & EICK
CINCINNATI

To our Cousin

Mrs. George S. Horner

Mutually beloved by the Author of these Poems, and by

C. A. P.

I have found a resource and comfort in the preparation of my husband's poems for collection and publication. They were mainly written in his early youth, and I read in them of his joys and sorrows, and of his faith, when the days of weariness came, in the higher life where all is light. This will be a very precious book if others can see it with my eyes. Whatever is not worthy belongs to the fond temerity of the gleaner.

C. A. PLIMPTON.

HE WHO HATH TOLD HIS MORTAL DAYS
AND PASSED BEYOND THE VOICE OF PRAISE,
FROM SONG'S FULL SERVICE WAS DEBARRED.
HE TOILSOME DAYS AND NIGHTS DID GUARD,
TO WHICH THE RECORDS IN THESE LEAVES
WERE WELCOME PERIODS AND REPRIEVES.
YET NONE THE LESS, IN HOUR OF NEED,
WITH GENEROUS FAITH HE BADE THEM SPEED,
WHO, HALF IN FEAR AND HOPEFUL HALF,
PIERIAN WATERS SOUGHT TO QUAFF.

EDITH M. THOMAS

MEMOIR.

FLORUS BEARDSLEY PLIMPTON was born September 4, 1830, in Palmyra, Portage Co., Ohio. His father, Billings O. Plimpton, who reached the age of ninety, and who died the day after the death of his son Florus, removed from Connecticut in the early part of the century, and connected himself with the Pittsburg Conference of the Methodist Episcopal Church, retaining an itinerant connection with it until the Erie Conference was erected, when he was set off with that branch of the itinerant work. He was one of the few, if not the last of the original members of that body. Shortly after entering upon his ministerial labors in Northern Ohio, he married Miss Eliza Merwin, youngest daughter of one of the early settlers of the Reserve.

Florus was the third son of this union. He received a common school and academic education, remaining on his father's farm in Hartford, Trumbull County, O., till seventeen years of age, when he entered Allegheny College, Meadville, Pa. In the spring of 1851 he connected himself with James Dumars in the publication of the Western Reserve Transcript at Warren, Trumbull County.

In the summer of 1852 he accepted an invitation to edit a Whig campaign paper at Niles, Mich. At the close of that political struggle he returned to Ohio, and was associated with John S. Herrick in conducting the Portage Whig, published at Ravenna. During his residence in this town he married Miss Cordelia A. Bushnell, of Hartford, Trumbull County, June 2, 1853. In the following spring he moved to Elmira, N. Y., where he was engaged until the spring of 1857 in the publication of the Elmira Daily Republican, and a weekly campaign paper in 1856. In 1857 he accepted a position in the city department of the Pittsburg Daily Dispatch, soon becoming one of its associate editors. In 1860 he became one of the staff of the Cincinnati Daily Commercial, and his labors with it and with the Commercial Gazette continued without interruption for a quarter of a century, and were of an unusually important character, breadth and responsibility. Late in 1885 he was prostrated by his first serious illness. He passed to rest April 23, 1886, deeply mourned by many loving friends, residing in almost every part of the Union. In accordance with his request, made a long period before his decease, his remains were cremated.

INTRODUCTION

By MURAT HALSTEAD.

SEVERAL times, during the quarter of a century in which we were associated in business and knew each other with intimacy, and shared in making up the estimates of current events that called for the mutual understanding of opinions and sympathies, Mr. Plimpton and myself were separated for weeks and months, sometimes with the Atlantic ocean between us, but we were never both long away from Cincinnati, and I find it most difficult to realize that he is on the journey to "The undiscovered country from whose bourn no traveller returns;" and when I absent myself from the office and come back, the old habit of enjoyment of his greeting asserts itself with surprising strength; and the consciousness that "the rest is silence" between us, strikes with a painful jar as it suddenly grows clear. We had so many things to think of together, and there were themes which I referred to him so constantly, that the custom of doing so seemed fixed; and still, as the endless duties of the occupation in which we were so closely engaged arise, I involuntarily appropriate his well remembered talents day after day, to perform the old tasks, forgetful for the moment that at last, and at least, "the weary are at rest."

Country boys, born in Ohio, with many kindred experiences and aspirations, hopes, themes, ambitions and disappointments, in early youth, we found ourselves when a little above the age of thirty years, on the same newspaper, subject to the limitations of an intelligent and inflexible authority—that of the controlling proprietor, M. D. Potter—and with unbounded opportunities for hard work. It happened that I had been something over seven years engaged in the Cincinnati Commercial Office, when Mr. Plimpton was introduced. He came to fill the situation that Mr. Potter always regarded the one most difficult to supply on the daily press—that of the writer of dramatic and musical criticism. How Mr. Plimpton came to be recommended in that capacity to Mr. Potter, I never knew or have totally forgotten. My recollection is distinct that Mr. Plimpton was immediately seen to be a quiet man, who did his work well and said very little about it. Presently there was observed in his paragraphs, a touch at once fine and forcible, and after a time, without noise or friction, his work grew in prominence and his position as a writer and one relied upon for good things formed itself. Without displacing or conflicting with any one he became a part of our force, and was at the front—no favors shown, but a favorite.

Abraham Lincoln was elected President, and the rising storm of Southern rebellion darkened the air. The Commercial Office had about three years before parted with Henry Reed, one of the strongest writers ever on the American press, and my own mind, that had been largely instructed in editorial duties under his influence, had not fully asserted itself in the expression of final opinions, and while I had gone into the Chase campaigns in Ohio, and the Fremont national campaign with zeal, Mr. Reed had held back and checked my enthusiasm with his conservative political philosophy. When he was gone, I found those about me going faster instead of slower in the popular current than I was disposed to go. Mr. Potter's general orders were very simple. The Commercial had to support the cause of free territories—which speedily became that of the free States.

As the discussion of the duty of the General Government in the presence of State rebellion progressed, and the various compromises and expedients looking to reconciliation were tested and found wanting—as the border State propositions, that those who had elected Lincoln should surrender, were found inapplicable, and the view that he should make his submission to the slave power, then rampant and threatening, was known to be inadmissible, and the theory that there should be a convention of all the States to make a permanent adjustment of difficulties, otherwise the peaceful separation of the conflicting sections, was seen to be as impossible as inexpedient, my associate in editorial labor was A. R. Spofford, who has long been librarian of Congress, and who held the pen of a very ready and strong writer, and while possessed of a vast fund of information, was wonderfully ready and accurate in quoting the teachings of history and the texts of literature.

The fact that Mr. Plimpton had very clearly defined opinions upon the questions of the day gradually became manifest to me, and I was the more interested because of the discovery that he was a more radical person than myself; that he believed in the application of the most thorough remedies for public wrongs and popular delusions. There was novelty in this. I had been accustomed to influences that pulled or pushed in the other direction. One remembrance is, that I, far more than others, believed from the first in the terrible earnestness of the Southern people. I was sure the South meant war, and the people of the North were exceedingly slow to reach that state of comprehension. My opportunities had, however, been better than those of any other man to know the state of the country, for I was the only one who saw the hanging of John Brown, and the exciting scenes of the following winter in Congress, which I studied from the gallery, and who attended the Democratic national and sectional conventions of 1860, in Charleston, Richmond and Baltimore.

The first pronounced opinion from Mr. Plimpton, dissenting from the course of the Commercial under my direction, was concerning a series of articles that suggested rather than advocated a convention of all the States, with the purpose of reaching a solution of sectional difficulties without war, even if the final result might be that the Slave States should, like "wayward sisters," as General Scott said, some months later, "depart in peace."

It did not occur to me that such a programme as this would be carried out. Of course there were insuperable difficulties. We had only to look closely into the situation to see that. But it was fashionable to propose ways and means for the avoidance of an appeal to arms, and this for a time seemed a possible diversion from the direct headlong, awful drift to war. The people of the North generally did not believe the South would fight. The Southern people held the like opinion of the North. I knew both were mistaken, and suggested the convention of all the States, and went so far as to say that the cotton would be as white and the wheat as golden, after the Slave States had set up for themselves, as before. This was not good politics, though it may not have been bad poetry, and I refer to it as marking the time I ascertained that the new man Plimpton was a well-read politician, a Republican in principle and of clear cut and resolutely held convictions.

More than once I have taken pleasure in saying that the mistakes in the management of the Cincinnati Commercial, while Mr. Plimpton and I were so closely associated, were mine, not his, and that errors of policy were usually, almost uniformly against his protest. He saw earlier and clearer and more constantly than I, the greatness of the figures in the war of Lincoln and Grant, and, whatever was true of others, had no prejudices to indulge against those who were faithful in the service of the imperiled country. I must confess that I was always slow to believe in new great men; and they came upon us in flocks in war time. There had to be a good deal accomplished besides the playing of Hail to the Chief by brass bands, before I could see the evidences that names until then but narrowly known, were to be blown across the whole world and into everlasting and overwhelming glory, by the trump of fame.

Mr. Plimpton's intuition, delicate as a woman's, was not unfrequently superior to my carefully weighed information and close calculation. He was in nothing, except his ever present integrity, more admirable than in his sense of humor, and his writings that are most pleasing are those that display the charming tints of his jovial fancy and the rippling lines of rhyme in which his fun became poetic. And yet there are but few examples of his touching serious subjects with a spirit of levity. There were many things in politics and religion that he had no talent for laughing at. He could not draw the fine lines so as to balance between declarations, and neither affirm nor deny, though it was not essential or important to pronounce for either; and he was not comfortable when it was the officially imposed duty to pose on the high and sharp fences of independent journalism; and personal journalism never was his pleasure.

His articles would commit the paper decidedly. The roads he traveled were always straight, and he was for or against Tom, Dick or Harry all the year round. The strength of conviction and keenness of purpose, that were his characteristics in combat, were too intense in him for a long course of badinage or a tedious policy of finesse. In public affairs he was nothing if not in earnest. In the first campaign of our prodigious and unwieldy military operations, Mr. Plimpton won his spurs as a war correspondent. He and Major Bickham contributed largely and acceptably to our columns from Western Virginia, but after this an unsuccessful attempt to be the historian of General Sherman's command in Kentucky, Sherman refusing to consent to the presence of representatives of the press, the work of the office grew in importance and demanded closer attention and more strenuous labors. The press was in a transition state, and the circulation and business generally of the newspapers increased rapidly, requiring changes in machinery and methods, and binding those employed in a round of cares ever enlarging and becoming more weighty and exacting. Mr. Plimpton's career as a war correspondent was closed—with the exception of an episode including his presence at the battle of Antietam—by the augmentation of the estimate placed upon the excellence of his editorial work; and when Mr. Spofford took practical charge of the library of Congress as first assistant, Mr. Plimpton's place became that of associate editor, and he held it "until his strength failed him at length."

We never had quarrels, but we had many differences. It was because we were unlike in our mental structure that we harmonized. My seven years in the office of the Commercial before he came, and the impression I had been able to make upon editorial labors and the acquirement of confidence and facility, gave me, as Mr. Potter's health, which had long been feeble, decisively declined, the first place of responsibility, and as is often the case, the Lieutenant did not invariably or even habitually see things along the same lines of light the Captain viewed them. Indeed it is often desirable that an object shall be observed from standpoints that make with it acute and even obtuse angles. Mr. Plimpton and I seldom were in direct antagonism in the consideration of a subject, but we often stood to it in such relations that if the right lines had been described there would have been drawn a right angled triangle.

Mr. Plimpton was incapable of intrigue or indirection. We always knew where he was, and what he meant and stood for. His integrity was so sure that there was no hesitation in trusting it; and in the delicate adjustments of the relations of the newspaper to individuals, and the complications of general and local matters, he was ever unselfish and faithful, rejecting opportunities to celebrate the things that were near to him personally, for the sake of preserving the traditions and the steady course of the common policy. This is hard to do sometimes, but the ground upon which it can be done is cleared, when we regard a great journal not so much an individual expression as a public institution and maintain its discipline for the preservation of its dignity.

The time of the work of Mr. Plimpton on the Cincinnati Commercial and the Commercial Gazette, was just about twenty-five years. He was well trained before he came, in North-eastern Ohio, in Elmira, New York, and in Pittsburg. His labors in Cincinnati extended over the most interesting period of the history of our country, and were addressed to the enlightenment of our constituency on a vast variety of subjects. Volumes of his writings might be selected from the files which form for each old established paper a library of its own; and there are veins of gold, that the historians who turn over the ample leaves upon which he wrote, will have need to appropriate for the fine metal of the coin of truth that is to circulate through the generations that will not, and indeed could not, search for themselves into the mass of newspaper literature.

Upon one subject Mr. Plimpton and myself were never quite serious; it was that of our literary productions when we were very young men; his ballads and my novelettes. We were a shade tender about those unconscious confessions of our youth. But we were so far from the days in which we first saw ourselves in print, as to be able to look as disinterested spectators upon our immature selves; and we respected, I am glad to say, the boys who had so early and fondly and foolishly fancied, they could do something for—even add to the romantic literature of the ideal West—the West that never was in the wilderness, and never will be in this world. I knew well long ago that while I should ask the forgiveness of forgetfulness for my crude Indian and rural stories, written to learn to write for the press, and out of want of occupation, there was something in the poetry of Plimpton that was rare and precious. Boy and man, through the changes of forty years he found in poetry the finer, higher, truer expression of himself. Loving hands have preserved with wonderful care that has rewarded itself, the poems that were the flowers of a life of labor always hard and often barren, and that was full of the inherent and impulsive qualities that are the springs of poetry—a life whose chief happiness was in the fervent faith that the earth was beautiful and mankind good.

In the collection that follows is one of those treasures that add to the riches that do not perish. No one can be so acutely sensitive to their imperfections as he was, whose heart and mind speak and sparkle in them. He valued them lightly because he was not a vain man, and they told of himself and had an inner radiance for him. He touched the harp because it comforted him. There were things to say that could not otherwise be said; there were tones, rays of light, to trace through melodies unheard by, and illuminations invisible to others—pathways into the infinite space that seemed to promise the divine achievement of the humanly unattainable. There are those who knew and loved him, certainly, and I believe many others, to whom these unostentatious utterances will be preferred to formal pomp and artificial splendor; and for the audience of the fit, whether many or few, they will be refreshing like a mountain rill or a bough laden with roses, or the flavor of the clover fields and tasseling corn, or the bloom of the locust and apple trees of Ohio. There is in them the glitter of those brighter things whose colors never fade, and the music that lingers forever of the better things, that are unsearchable save by those whose gift is to put on the wings of poetry.

MURAT HALSTEAD.

Cincinnati, Sept. 10th, 1886.

REMARKS OF GEN'L J. D. COX

AT THE OBSEQUIES OF MR. F. B. PLIMPTON, CINCINNATI, APRIL 25, 1886.

I HAVE been requested to say a few words in regard to our departed friend, and as I reflect upon what I ought to say, I am impressed more than one often can be with the way in which the past and the present sometimes link themselves together.

Both Florus Plimpton and myself have been too busy men in our different spheres of work to be very often thrown together. For many years our interviews, though warmly friendly, have necessarily been brief, and therefore, when I was asked to say something about him, I naturally thought of that time which now seems a long way off, when he and I were young men together.

We began life, I in my profession, he in his, in a little town in the northern part of the State, when we were both just beyond our boyhood, both full of hopes, and both earnest in our own plans for work; and yet it so happened that we were thrown for a time quite closely together. He was full of that literary spirit which never left him, but which, in his early manhood, probably had a stronger hold upon him, and made more of his life and character than it could afterward.

Full of poetic dreams, full of strong purpose, and embodying it in worthy literary work, yet he was already committed to that laborious career, as editor of a journal, to which his working days and nights had to be devoted. I naturally looked back, as I said, to that time, thinking of him as I saw him then, and when yesterday I took his son by the hand, it seemed to me as though he had grown to manhood almost while we had been thinking, or that it was his father as he stood before me thirty years ago that I so well remembered. It is this bringing of the past and present together that sometimes comes upon us almost with a shock. The gap between has been full of interest to us both. The plans we laid out were very far indeed, perhaps, from being those we either of us followed, and yet, looking back on that life, I think we can not help saying that, in his case, it has been full of wonderful fruit of its own; full of a character that was ever ripening; full of maturing growth of that power of intellect and of imagination which he showed as a boy.

He would have been glad could he have made his life essentially and purely a literary one, essentially and purely a poetic one. I have no doubt that was his earliest longing, but with courage and with determination he recognized fairly the fact that the poetic is only a small part of any man's life; that there are rare chances, few and far between, when a man can wholly follow out the imaginative desires of his heart and mind. There was work to do, and to that work he addressed himself, whatever leisure moments his arduous task granted being devoted to what was beautiful in nature and art. He did not blink the truth that in this busy, every-day world the work of the day is really that to which every man and woman must give most of their time and most of their strength.

To that, therefore, he devoted himself with the zeal and power which others are more competent to speak of than am I, for of the work of modern journalism, of those who devote their time and mind to the unending task of editing a daily newspaper, we know little. Knowing what I know, seeing what I have seen in these kindly touches of the elbow when marching through life, in these memories of the friendship of early days, I can testify that the man's power was ripening and strengthening in life and constantly beautifying it as he went on to its close.

I can not help thinking it would be hard to find a life that in many respects is a purer, a more desirable one, than that which our friend lived.

He devoted himself to thinking out those problems affecting the interests of the whole world, which are every day arising, and by his pen laid them before the eyes of men. He did not do it ostentatiously—the very character of his work made it a quiet one. Not seeking the glory of a public life—indeed quite aside from it, working away, day after day, night after night, putting his thought into such form that the intellect of the people of his time might profit by it, and now, during that thirty-odd years of that sort of labor, what may be really thought of the accomplishment? How much has been done we can imagine better than we can know. Starting from these early days, in the '50's, we know that great things were being agitated in our midst. Hearts were stirred with the suspicion of coming revolution. One of those great events which mark an epoch and which has made our age memorable to all ages, was coming to the surface. From that on, during all this period, his mind and pen labored unremittingly for the press, and he has contributed much to make our country what it is.

All these things occur to us naturally, and I am glad of the opportunity to say, in this brief way, how it has impressed me; and judging of it, as his early friends might judge, I feel, when we come to put him away, that his has been a life well-spent; a life which, both for its happiness and accomplishment, has been well worth the living. Then when we add to it his excursions into that field to which he constantly turned—the love of art, the love of poetry, of nature, and of all that is beautiful in the world—we see the beauty of the life of our friend. We who have known him know the purity of his life—his adherence to what he believed was right—the singleness of purpose with which he followed what he thought was true.

I believe those who know him best believe he has fairly worked out his allotted days according to the power that was in him. He has not spared himself, and in doing this he has, perhaps, accomplished more than could have been done during a longer life.

To those near and dear to him, and to all his friends, year after year, his memory will only grow the riper and richer. There is nothing to look back upon with shame or fear in the life of our friend. As all these events of his life get a little further into the past they will glow with the halo of the light of all he has done, with the beautiful effects of distance tending to make us appreciate them more than when they were close to us, and making us better understand what the man was in his character and purpose. I think we and they have the right to feel this. The memory of his life to all who knew him will be a constant stimulus to be worthy of the friendship of such a man.

TRIBUTES FROM ASSOCIATE JOURNALISTS.

THE following, written by a fellow worker with Mr. Plimpton for twenty-five years, appeared in the Commercial Gazette, April 24, 1886.

There was that in Mr. Plimpton that was quite untamable for empty worldly uses. His sense of honor was the keenest; a mean act called forth his quick resentment. He entered no scramble for advancement; intrigue he abhorred. His character was totally free from disguise. Deceit in others shocked him, and he was slow to give it that name. He was sensitive, yet a spirit of revenge was totally foreign to him. He was a man of infinite quiet jest, of infinite appreciation of the beautiful and of art, a friend of his kind, a cheerful and resolute soldier of duty. His generosity to the unfortunate was noted, and he did not turn away from those whose misfortunes were self-inflicted. In public affairs his feelings were as warm as his labors were earnest. His patriotism was an energetic sentiment. Those who enjoyed his friendship recognized in him a companion of rare accomplishments and a fineness of qualities that they will not meet with again in the same lovable combination. There is, in our opinion, no man living who can say that he was wronged in act or thought by Mr. Plimpton. His record is finished, and no one can step forth to point out a questionable deed, or a word of malice. He loved the world and its beauties, its creatures and its responsibilities, and his neighbor as himself. He brightened his wide circle while here; and his departure leaves a clear and steady ray for remembrance.

Mr. Plimpton was a born poet. To devote himself to poetry would doubtless have been the ideal life for him. There was about him at times a poetic abstraction that his associates understood, and often, after the paper went to press, at 3 or 4 o'clock in the morning, he would write two or three stanzas on a subject that had at some time of the busy day flashed into his mind, and had been put aside to wait for a moment of leisure. These poetic subjects were most varied. He did not seek to control them, nor reduce them to any system. Generally they were left unfinished; yet they forced a hearing since he could not resist them entirely. Sometimes he would repeat to an intimate friend a couplet that had darted into his mind ready made, and he would complete the stanza, giving it more than likely an amusing turn. Vigorous as he was in the prose of journalism, and great as were his resources as a writer of masculine leaders and paragraphs with the keenest edge, he yet impressed those who knew him well as one who would never cease to feel the fascinations of poetry and belles lettres.

Mr. Plimpton began to write poetry as a boy. He contributed poems to various newspapers and periodicals—the Knickerbocker Magazine, Godey's Lady's Book, Genius of the West, New York Tribune, Ohio State Journal, and Cincinnati Commercial. His poetry is graceful and gentle, the reflex of happy moods, or of tender seriousness. It is characterized by an intense love of natural scenery, especially far-reaching pastoral or forest loveliness. He was master, too, of the pathos that is twixt a smile and a tear, as evidenced by such poems as that in which the poor homeless woman, in her misery, beseeches His Honor to make her sentence four months instead of two. His lines are very musical, and owe their melody to an inborn sense of rhythm. His poems—of which he was himself so careless—should now be collected. They will give him a place of honor among Ohio singers.

He was not willing, however, to collect them himself, for he was of a retiring spirit, and he saw in them youthful imperfections of art, or failure, in maturer years, to reach his own ideals or full intent. The poems are widely scattered in newspapers and magazines, and many of them can only be recovered by patient search. He never contemplated their publication in a volume; but those who are familiar with even a few of them know that their author underrated their quality, and regarded the subject of their collection too lightly:

> "Poets are all who love, who feel great truths,
> And tell them; and the truth of truths is love."

J. W. M.

IN venturing a few comments on Florus B. Plimpton's literary character, I am happily aided by the impressions of personal acquaintance and friendship lasting through a series of years, and becoming somewhat close and intimate towards the end of his life. I may say that I had an impressive touch of his literary judgment at our first meeting, which was when he happened to be temporarily in charge of a great daily newspaper, and I the latest addition to the staff of local reporters. It was then that he took pains to check my youthful ardor on entering the field of journalism, telling me that success lay not so much in enthusiasm and flights of fancy as in patience and plain work. At a later day he was more emphatic in declaring that if I hoped to get on well with the paper I must abandon my poetry (which I confess was not good), and stick to everyday prose. The advice, though cold and hard, went home with great force, for he was a poet of acknowledged merit, and an accomplished literary critic, as well as an experienced and practical journalist. However, I owe him a great debt of gratitude for kindly words of encouragement when I felt I sorely needed them, but could not solicit them anywhere.

He was generously disposed towards young writers of whom many came to him for advice, carefully entering into the details of their plans, directing the progress of their work, writing introductions for their books, and assisting them in many ways. As to his own compositions, the mass of them of course went into the anonymous columns of the newspaper, to be turned to the gaze of the world for a day, and then to the dusty wall forever. While the poetic sentiment was strong within him, and its expression most happy, he almost to the point of total suppression subordinated the gentle muse to the rigorous requirements of his business tasks. Thus happen so many fragments and unfinished pieces among the few complete poems he has left to us. At times, when in perfect mood, and the idle moments dragged, he would dash off a few lines of a poem in his mind, and, suddenly interrupted by a summoning duty, thrust the manuscript, ink-wet and blotted, into his desk to be forgotten with the vanished inspiration. In after days, when clearing out the dusty pigeon-holes, he would come across these fugitives, read them to a friend who might be near, joke upon them and throw them into the waste basket—a few exceptions being stowed away again, to be "finished up some day," or, more likely, cast aside at the next overhauling. Distinguished for his intelligence and appreciation in high art and literature, Mr. Plimpton was still very fond of indulging his taste for homely country themes, and of calling up memories of boyhood amid gentle surroundings. There were at least two or three of his ballads, unfinished and long ago lost, I suppose, which for sweetness and tenderness were hardly excelled by Phoebe Cary's famous "Old Brown Homestead" that

> "Reared its walls
> From the wayside dust aloof,
> Where the apple boughs could almost cast
> Their fruitage on the roof."

However much we may prize Mr. Plimpton's more elaborate poems, carefully constructed and polished for formal occasions, and which in my humble judgment are not his best; however much we may enjoy his songs and narrative verses; however fondly we may gather up the loose fragments, glad in our regret at their unfinished state that the fragments themselves at least remain to us, who will attempt to estimate the number and quality of the poems of his composition that shall never see the light of print—not even the light of manuscript? It was his habit in the evening to leave his study in the newspaper office and saunter about the streets of the city for exercise and fresh air. Frequently in his strolls he would compose a complete poem of several stanzas, which he would bring back in his mind, recite perhaps to the first person he met at the office—and that was the end of it.

Mr. Plimpton wrote his last poem in November, 1885, after a long night's work. Living in the suburbs, it was his custom to remain in the office until daylight, and then take a street car for his home. I had asked him to contribute something for a little magazine of which I was the editor. One morning on coming to the office, I found the poem as he had left it on my desk. He had written it in the silent hours after the other newspaper people had gone, and he was in the great building entirely alone. He entitled it "Bereaved," and it certainly breathes the spirit of sorrow and desolation, if not of utter despair. This was at a time when Mr. Plimpton was suffering intensely, and rapidly losing strength under the disease that in a few months caused his death.

J. M. C.

Cincinnati, Oct. 28, 1886.

ILLUSTRATIONS

· BY ·

Prof. J. W. Shirmer, (deceased)	
Prof. Hans Gude,	BERLIN
Prof. Wm. Riefstahl,	MUNICH
C. T. Webber,	CINCINNATI
E. D. Grafton,	"
Henry Mosler,	PARIS
Chas. Niehaus,	ROME
C. A. Fries,	CINCINNATI
L. C. Weglau,	"
H. F. Farny,	"
L. F. Plympton,	"
A. R. Valentine,	"
Miss C. Newton,	
Miss Laura Fry,	"
Miss M. Spencer,	
Mrs. A. B. Merriam,	
Mrs. C. A. Plimpton,	"

Reproductions by the Heliotype Printing Co., Boston
Moss Engraving Co., New York.

Contents.

	PAGE.
The Oak,	1
Souvenirs,	7
The Poet's Habitation,	10
In Dreams of Heaven,	13
Lewis Wetzel,	14
Content,	20
The Nobly Great,	21
Prayer of Old Age,	23
Evening Hymn,	24
Christus Sylvæ,	25
The Cricket,	29
The Universal Robber,	31
The Reformer,	32
Fort Du Quesne	35

CONTENTS.

Ode,	38
Pittsburg,	40
Sonnet,	41
Mount Gilbo,	42
Hermit of Mount Gilbo,	45
A Woman's Tear,	51
A Poor Man's Thanksgiving,	52
En Memoire,	53
Our Country's Flag,	57
Love's Heralds,	58
Heaven's Evangels,	59
Ossian to His Harp,	60
Tell Me True,	62
The Hero of the Arctic,	64
Why Mourn, O Friend,	66
Star of the Evening,	67
Make it Four, Yer Honor,	69
The Brown Chick-a-dee,	72
The Two Mariners,	73
The Emigrant's Invitation,	74
From Their Serene Abodes,	75
The Morning Prayer,	77
Philo is Dead,	79
Her Record,	81
Sleigh-Ride Song,	82
Waiting,	83
In Remembrance,	87
Spiritus Sylvæ,	89
Bereaved,	96
There Comes a Time,	97
The Rural Editor,	99
In Memory,	108
A New Year's Rhyme,	110
The Farmer,	115
By the Sea-Side,	116
Sonnet,	118

The Fountain in the Wilderness,	119
The Unreturning,	125
As I Love,	126
Morning on Maryland Heights,	127
Summer Days,	131
A Suburban Home,	133
The Avowal,	135
Protean Dust,	136
The Early Dead,	137
A Retrospect,	139
Home,	140
Ellula,	143
The Flower Angels,	145
Waiting to Die,	146
The Loved Ones Afar,	149
October,	150
The Unsealed Future,	151
Song of Parting,	152
Pio Nono,	153
For His Mercy Endureth Forever,	155

POEMS

THE OAK.

GRANDLY apart the giant monarch stands,
All reverend with lichens, looking down
A green declivity on pastoral lands,
And all the waysides choke with dust and heat,
Beneath the shadow of his regal crown,
Fair maids and lusty youth at eve retreat,
To dance the hours away with lightly-twinkling feet.

When, to the singing of the early birds,
Spring bursts in blossoms from the southern sky,
And scornful of the stall, the lowing herds
In pastures green delight to graze and lie;
When milk-white doves to mossy gables fly—
Heaven filled with song, earth with sweet utterings,
And winds through odorous vales blow pleasantly,
Its thousand boughs seem bursting into wings,
Silken and smooth and green and full of flutterings.

THE OAK.

Among thick drapery of green its nest
The dormouse builds, and there the robins sing,
Till Evening sets her roses in the west.
On topmost boughs the chattering squirrels swing,
And round its twigs the spiders spin and cling
Their gauzy nets; there too the beetles creep
To hide in shaggy cells, where wood-ticks ring
Their mid-watch bells while weary mortals sleep—
What time, 'tis said, the elves their mystic revels keep.

Here, ancients say, his royal brothers stood;
But none remains—the giant stands alone,
The gracious lord of the primeval wood,
The hoary monarch of an heirless throne.
Here, when the summer's glory gilds its own,
And day dims dying in the purple air,
The angels come and wake each heavenly tone
That floats around and fondly lingers there—
A wordless song of praise from murmuring lips of prayer.

Or when capricious autumn dyes with hues
Crimson and brown and gold, this forest Lear,
And spangles of the hoar-frost and the dews
Like countless brilliants flash afar and near
The gorgeous state he keeps; and cold and clear,
The subtle arrows of quick-quivering light
With luster tip the leaves now crisp and sere,
Then seems the oak th' enchantment of the night,
A splendor of weird spells, a cheat upon the sight!

But most 'tis kingly when the laboring woods
With gusty winds and darkening tempests roar,
And crash the thunders of the seething floods
That snow their white foam on the wrecking shore;
When Winter rages on the lonely moor,

Yokes the swift whirlwind to his icy car,
And in Titanic folds the heavens o'er,
Gathers his cloudy banners from afar,
And marshals with shrill blasts the elements to war.

O then the sound of the entangled wind,
Among its boughs, is like the stormy swell
Of organ-pipes in fretted walls confined,
To roll through arches vast and die in vault and cell.
How like the grand old monarch, when the fell
And pitiless storm seemed with the world to mock
His uncrown'd age—and yet how strong and well
It braved the storm and bore the tempest's shock,
Firm in its native soil as alpine rock to rock.

And well I love that oak! Not those that shade
Thy classic slopes, Mount Ida; or shake down
Their brown-hued fruit, from gnarlèd boles decayed,
Beside the winding Simois; or crown
The horrid steeps where ivied castles frown,
And dark-eyed bandits bid th' unwary stand;
Are regal in their centuries of renown
As thou, hale oak, whose glories thus command
My humble song, O pride of all our mountain land!

Here rests the poor wayfarer, soiled and worn,
And folds his hands in slumbers soft and deep;
Here comes the widowed soul her loss to mourn,
Counts o'er her trysts, and counts them but to weep;
Here happy lovers blissful unions keep,
And bending age its vanished youth deplores,
Or sighs for heaven's sweet rest, life's gentlest sleep,
That gives youth back to age, the lost restores,
And brings the welcoming hands that waft to happier shores.

The village maid, who sings among the fields,
In wrinkled sorrow sighs her soul away;
The dimpled babe to reverend honors yields,
And patriarch Faith sees calmly close the day.
Life laughs — loves — dies; afar the years convey
On cloudy wings the pleasures we pursue,
And still thou piercest the repelling clay,
And lift'st thy regal head to heaven's blue,
Green with a thousand years of sunshine, rain and dew.

In all thy varied glory thou hast been
The idol of my boyhood, and the pride
Of more exacting manhood; now, as then,
I love to lean thy moss-green trunk beside,
And mingle, with the voices of the tide
And thy strange whisperings, my unstudied song,
And here recall the dear delights who died
Since thy great arms grew obstinately strong —
But whose quick feet no more beneath thy shade shall throng.

SOUVENIRS.

I.—L'ENVOY.

AS sweetly tranced the ravished Florentine
    Tarried 'mid pallid gloom, again to hear
    Cassella warble tuneful to his ear,
Thus I, a Bacchant, rosy with love's wine,
Drink thy words, sweet, forgetful with what haste
    Time's wingèd heel beats rearward all the hours.
    To me alike all seasons, deeds and powers,
When by the atmosphere of love embraced,
I sit sun-crowned, and as a god elate,
  In thy dear presence. Let the great world go.
  In lowliest meads the pansies love to grow,
And sweet Content was born to low estate.
Here is our blessed Egeria—let us stay:
Where love has fixed the heart, no charm can lure away.

II.—TELL HER.

RIVER Beautiful! the breezy hills
   That slope their green declivities to thee,
   In purple reaches hide my life from me.
Go then, beyond the thunder of the mills,
And wheels that churn thy waters into foam,
   And murmuring softly to the darling's ear,
   And murmuring sweetly when my love shall hear,
Tell how I miss her presence in our home.
Say that it is as lonely as my heart;
   The rooms deserted; all her pet birds mute;
   The sweet geraniums odorless; the flute
Its stops untouched, while wondrous gems of art
Lie lusterless as diamonds in a mine,
To kindle in her smile and in her radiance shine.

SOUVENIRS.

III.—RETURN.

RETURN—return! nor longer stay thy feet,
   Where rugged hills shut in the peaceful dale,
   And chattering runnels riot through the vale,
And lose themselves in meadows violet sweet.
Or does the oriole charm thee; or the lark
   Lure thee to green fields, where the gurgling brook
   Leaps up to kiss thy feet, the while we look
For thee with tearful eyes from morn till dark?
O winds, that blow from out th' inconstant west,
   O birds, that eastward wing your heavenly way,
   Tell her of our impatience—her delay,
And woo the wanderer to her humble nest;
Come, as the dove that folds her wings in rest,
When holy evening sets her watch-star in the west.

THE POET'S HABITATION.

HE Poet's habitation is the World;
And his most sacred thoughts become its own.
He is the interpreter of the natural earth,
And gives inanimate substances a voice
And subtlety of language, which do make
Them sybils to the restless heart of man—
Confessors to its secret questionings;
And he delights in solitude to dwell,
'Mid grey-cloaked crags, around whose loveless fronts,
Like Firmness baring to the sport of Fate,
Frosty Euroclydon and Boreas gruff
Hoarsely and harshly howl their discontent.
Mountains that, grandly rising, prop the sky,
Inaccessible ravines and forests dark,
The solemn sounding sea and lonely shore,
Desert and moor, and melancholy haunt,
The grave, the silent, vast, profound, sublime,
Are to his spirit, in their loneliness,
Th' unerring teachings of a hidden POWER.
He revels in the storm; and in the roar
Of sulphurous thunder, and the fearful pulse
Of troubled waters beating on the shore,
He hears the anthem of a Universe
To the INVISIBLE.

        In his milder moods
He seeks the quiet of the templed grove,
Or the untrammeled glen, that human art
Hath not despoiled of natural loveliness.

Th' enameled banks that hem the gurgling brook—
Whose crystal waters with the scent of mint,
And roses wild (whose petaled blushes fall,
And glide, like pleasures in our childhood,
So gently down the stream) are redolent—
Those banks, where tender flocks their gambols take,
Sweet with the breath of violets and anemones,
And of the wild-pea, sweetest child of spring;
The willow copse that bends its tassel'd boughs
To the least breathing of the gentle South;
And the old oaks that spread their generous limbs
As cool retreats 'gainst June's meridian sun,—
These, with the outlines of such pastoral scene,
Swelling and blending with the softest grace,
Like woman's beauty, to his dreamy eye
Are a perpetual delight and joy.

To him no music sweeter than the songs of birds,
Or childhood's artless utterance
Of joys wild gushing through its bounding heart;
Or the low carol of a love-born song,
By maiden lips, beneath an evening sky,
Sung with fresh orals to the ear of Love;
Or plaints of lucid fountains, or the chimes
Of distant church-bells dying on the air,
That leave, like kind farewell words, within the heart
A most delicious calm of pensive joy.

And when retiring fades the jocund day—
When sable-hooded twilight, like old age
That wraps itself in shadows, cometh on,
And shuts from vision all external things
(As sleep the senses from the outer world)—
When, even as diamonds set in sapphire, blaze
In the cerulean all the hosts of heaven—

Forever young-eyed watchers o'er old earth—
His silver-slippered Fancy calls to life
Th' innumerable fairies of the sylvan shade,
Peoples the founts and streams with dew-eyed nymphs,
And to their revels by the moon-light calls
Pale Fay and timid Fawn and laughing Puck,
And give to silence and to solitude
A thousand denizens of purity.

IN DREAMS OF HEAVEN.

In dreams of Heaven I see thy face,
    Divinely sweet, divinely fair;
No stain of earth hath left its trace
    To mar the fadeless beauties there,
But calm and pure its high repose,
    And fresher than the morning rose.

I wake, and lo! the vision fled,
    Leaves doubt and dark'ning thought behind;
Shall I, when numbered with the dead,
    Thy radiant beauty seek and find,
And walk beside thee, hand in hand,
The fair fields of the better land?

Yet gentle spirit, oft thine eyes
    Must fill with tears as they survey
A scene where every pleasure dies,
    Where loves grow cold, and hopes decay,
And life, however bright and blest,
Ends in the one desire for rest.

LEWIS WETZEL.*

I.

Stout-hearted Lewis Wetzel
Rides down the river shore,
The wilderness behind him,
And the wilderness before.

He rides in the cool of morning,
Humming a dear old tune,
Into the heart of the greenwood,
Into the heart of June.

He needs no guide in the forest,
More than the hunter bees;
His guides are the cool green mosses
To the northward of the trees.

---

* Lewis Wetzel was a "mighty hunter" in the pioneer days of Western Virginia, of which he was a native. Many traditionary anecdotes of his extraordinary skill with the rifle are yet preserved, some of which have been published. An imperfect sketch of his life is given in Dr. Doddridge's "Notes on the Settlement and Indian Wars in the Western parts of Virginia and Pennsylvania."

Nor fears he the foe whose footstep
   Is light as the summer air—
The tomahawk hangs in his shirt-belt,
   And the scalpknife glitters there!

The stealthy Wyandots tremble,
   And speak his name with fear,
For his aim is sharp and deadly,
   And his rifle's ring is clear.

So, pleasantly rides he onward,
   Pausing to hear the stroke
Of the settler's axe in the forest,
   Or the crash of a falling oak;

Pausing at times to gather
   The wild fruit overhead;
(For in this rarest of June days
   The service-berries are red);

And as he grasps the full boughs,
   To bend them down amain,
The dew and the blushing berries
   Fall like an April rain.

The partridge drums on the dry oak,
   The croaking corby caws,
The blackbird sings in the spice-bush,
   And the robin in the haws;

And, as they chatter and twitter,
   The wild birds seem to say,
"Do not harm us, good Lewis,
   And you shall have luck to-day."

So, pleasantly rides he onward,
  Till the shadows mark the noon,
Into the leafy greenwood,
  Into the heart of June.

II.

Now speed thee on, good Lewis,
  For the sultry sun goes down,
The hill-side shadows lengthen,
  And the eastern sky is brown.

Now speed thee where the river
  Creeps slow in the coverts cool,
And the lilies nod their white bells
  By the margin of the pool.

He crosses the silver Kaska
  With its chestnut-covered hills,
And the fetlocks of his roan steed
  Are wet in a hundred rills.

"And there," he cries in transport,
  "The alders greenest grow,
Where the wild stag comes for water,
  And her young fawn leads the doe."

Grasping his trusty rifle,
  He whistles his dog behind,
Then stretches his finger upward
  To know how sets the wind.†

---

† It was a custom among pioneer hunters (says Doddridge), when on hunting expeditions, and in the vicinity of favorite hunting grounds, to thrust the forefinger into the mouth, and when heated, to hold it out into the air. By this means they readily detected the course of the wind.

O! steady grows the strong arm,
   And the hunter's dark eye keen,
As he sees the branching antlers
   Through the alder thickets green.

A sharp, clear ring through the greenwood,
   And with mighty leap and bound,
The pride of the western forest
   Lies bleeding on the ground.

Then out from the leafy shadow
   A stalwart hunter springs,
And his unsheathed scalpknife glittering
   Against his rifle rings.

"And who are you," quoth Lewis,
   "That com'st 'twixt me and mine?"
And his cheek is flushed with anger,
   As a bacchant's flushed with wine.

"What boots that to thy purpose?"
   The stranger hot replies;
"My rifle marked it living,
   And mine when dead the prize."

Then with sinewy arms they grapple,
   Like giants fierce in brawls,
Till stretched along the greensward
   The humbled hunter falls.

Upspringing like a panther,
   He cries in wrath and pride,
"Though your arms may be the stronger,
   Our rifles shall decide."

"Stay, stranger," quoth good Lewis,
  "The chances are not even;
Who challenges my rifle
  Should be at peace with heaven.

"Now take this rod of alder,
  Set it by yonder tree,
A hundred yards beyond me,
  And wait you there and see.

"For he who dares such peril
  But lightly holds his breath;
May his unshrived soul be ready
  To welcome sudden death!"

So the stranger takes the alder,
  And wondering stands to view,
While Wetzel's aim grows steady,
  And he cuts the rod in two.

"By Heavens!" the stranger shouted,
  "One only, far or nigh,
Hath arms like the lithe young ash-tree,
  Or half so keen an eye;

And that is Lewis Wetzel:"
  Quoth Lewis, "Here he stands;"
So they speak in gentler manner,
  And clasp their friendly hands.

Then talk the mighty hunters
  Till the summer dew descends,
And they who met as foemen
  Ride out of the greenwood friends;—

Ride out of the leafy greenwood
  As rises the yellow moon,
And the purple hills lie pleasantly
  In the softened air of June.

CONTENT.

IN this decaying leaf,
    And that bright scarlet berry,
I read of times for grief
    And seasons to be merry.

Go, then, thy cheerful ways,
    To sup with joy or sorrow,
Hope with fair Youth to-day,
    And dream with Age to-morrow.

For God be thanked, who fills
    The world with light and shadow,
Puts strength across the hills
    And beauty in the meadow.

He knows our varying ways,
    Their bitterness and sweetness,
And gives to wholesome days
    Their measure of completeness.

Thus singing will I go,
    Nor count my gains or losses,
And bear, as best I know,
    The burden of my crosses.

And this my only creed
    In hours of doubt and blindness.
Who sows for human need
    Shall reap in human kindness.

THE NOBLY GREAT.

NONE but the good are nobly great!
    To him will justice yield the prize
    Who seeks to better man's estate,
    And render earth a paradise.
    What though the brow be stellate with the gems
  Of royal bounty, or the civic wreath
Weave its green honors 'mid Narcissian curls,
  If the high soul beneath
Purple the luster of those diadems
With thoughts of blood, that over groaning worlds
Would stride to power, nor fear the bold essay,
Though human hearts should pave the slippery way!
When Death shall smite the scepter of such power,
  And the gray sexton hide his human clay;
When, like the vision of an idle hour,
  Shall pass the glory of his strength away,
Like a dark shadow, through the coming years
  Shall the remembrance of his deeds extend,
And they who praised, when vengeance roused their fears,
  Refuse to own that he was once their friend.
Beside his grave shall watch hand-hidden shame,
  And Infamy around it stalk in gloom;
Just curses fall, like blight, upon his name,
  And Hate disturb the ashes of his tomb.

THE NOBLY GREAT.

He who would stand among
The great celestials canonized by Love—
  Truth's hero-gods and bards of holy song—
  And shine, a glory, 'mid that mighty throng,
Must noble deeds by noble aims approve.
It matters not how lowly be his birth,
  How poor his garb, or humble be his aim;
Love, Truth and Justice stamp the man of worth,
  And yield the homage of enduring fame.

The marble crumbles; monuments decay,
  And brazen statues topple to their fall;
Time eats the hardest adamant away,
  And cold Oblivion mars the pride of all.
But he who graces every act with love,
  Or stamps a thought with th' impress of truth,
  Twines laureled honors of perpetual youth
Around his brow, and life in duty spent,
Builds in the hearts of men a monument
Which Hate or Time will vainly strive to move.

PRAYER OF OLD AGE.

OH Time! deal gently with us—let us go
   As peaceful to our rest as summer's bird,
  When lulled by evening winds and tinkling flow
Of rock-born fountains. In our hearts are stirred
Dear memories of the days of long ago,
   Affection's look and love's endearing word.
O kindly lead earth's pilgrims by the hand
To the calm portals of the Silent Land.

EVENING HYMN.

ER the craggy mountains pealing,
    Listen to the vesper bell,
Softly o'er the waters stealing,
    Heavenly peace its tones foretell.
Father, up in heaven above us,
Deign to pardon, bless and love us;
    Guard us ever,
    Keep us ever
From all ill while here we dwell.

As the sun shines on the ocean,
    Ere it leaves our happy skies,
Smile upon our heart's devotion—
    Let our praise to Thee arise.
For the sins to us forgiven,
For the peace we have from heaven,
    Holy Father,
    Blessèd Father,
Let our praise to Thee arise.

Now the evening star revealing,
    Shines upon retiring day,
And the purple tints are stealing
    From the mountain tops away.
Be Thy love our star of guidance,
When age dims life's cheerful radiance,
    Keep us near Thee,
    Ever near Thee—
Never let us go astray.

CHRISTUS SYLVAE.

I.

THE lizard and the water snake,
    All things that haunt in tarn and brake,
Are bred where, fretting through its flags,
The sluggish Pymatuning lags;
The winds grow heavy as with death,
(So do they feel the poisonous breath
Of snaky vines, green spume of sedge
And fern that fringe the river's edge),
Swoon where the waters darkly pass
Stained with the stain of bruiséd grass,
Roots of dead things, and leaves the years
Have scorched with fires and steeped in tears.

Broad flats there are to left and right:
A wilderness whose mystic shades
Nor light is seen nor moon invades,
Where fear the startled foot makes light
As steps among damp graves at night.
From tangled undergrowth uprise
Thick-fruited beeches, hickories,
Elms pendulous and walnuts hoar.
The ghostly-armored sycamore,
And rugged oaks from whose green cowls
Hoot the long night the hooded owls.

II.

Drawn strangely to this solitude
Came one whom no man understood.
Painter and sculptor, he had wrought
In outward form his inward thought,
Whereof the meaning dimly guessed
The rude who stared and round him pressed.
They knew what flocks were best afield,
What lands could fattest harvests yield;
Seasons they knew and times, but not
The painter's dream, the sculptor's thought,
And whispered, when they passed him by,
"Hist! he hath madness in his eye."

Careless of good report or ill,
He wrought with hand of patient skill
In line and shade and form to tell
A tale of tales most wonderful—
How, touched with sorrow for our state,
Heaven opened wide its pearly gate
And One, to wound our sinful pride,
Descended, prayed for us and died.
One face upon his canvas shone,
One face he carved in wood and stone,
Wherein great pity was and love
And suffering, the heart to move;
Yet so divine its gracious air
That women came and worshipped there,
And men, who thought to scoff and jeer,
Turned to wipe off th' unbidden tear.

But he the artist, was as one
Who in a language not his own,
Strives to make clear the laboring sense:

Or one who hears in holy hours
Voices that seem from native land—
The angels singing 'mid the flowers—
Hears them but can not understand;
And though unskilled on instruments
Yet seeks to utter through the keys
The burden of their melodies;
So trying, oft, as oft in vain,
To shape the image of his brain,
With troubled countenance he cried
"Unsatisfied, unsatisfied!"
And in great grief none understood,
Withdrew him to the solitude.

III.

"Lord Christ!" he prayed, hand smiting hand,
In the dark shadow of the land,
"As thou didst show thyself to her
Who waited at the sepulchre,
Once more reveal thyself to sight,
And out of darkness bring the light.
Make clear my inward sense of Thee—
Love, softening, heavenly majesty,
Grace, shining through a cloud of pain,
Patience to bear and not complain,
Forgiveness, conquering sense of wrong,
And pity for a scoffing throng.
So shall these hands obedient trace
The features of no mortal face,
And men shall say, "Behold how fair—
The presence of a God is there!"

And still he prayed: "Lord! Thou art here
Embracing as the atmosphere.
Thy love the wood-birds' notes confess,

The simple flower thy tenderness;
Thou walkest in the wilderness.
So will I carve my thought of Thee
And fashion from the living tree;
In Thine own temple shall it stand,
O'erlooking all the lovely land,
And men shall say, approaching near,
Behold, our Father dwelleth here.

IV.

So said, from out fair ranks of trees
He chose—for sweetness stung by bees—
One whose green tops the morning sun
Was first of trees to look upon.
The fragrant boughs he lopped: it stood
Bare as when winters scourge the wood,
Or lightnings rive, or tongues of fire
Outrun the winds in keen desire.
Then wrought in saintly solitude
This man whom no man understood,
And through the silence of the air
At evening rose the solemn prayer,
"In thine own temple, Lord appear!"

When frosts make silvery every sound,
And scarlet trumpets fire the ground,
Two hunters, wandering through the wood,
Saw with awed eyes and understood.
Prone at the carved trees gnarlèd face,
One dead they saw, and shivering there,
Clear in the crystal of the air,
A face that seemed no mortal face—
The presence of a God was there!

THE CRICKET

WHEN shrill the icy winds of winter sing,
  The harsh hail rattling madly at the door,
  And thought goes shivering for the houseless poor
Who feel the bitter blast and biting sting—
If closer to my fireside then I cling,
  And hear from out the hollow of the hearth
  The comfortable cricket chirp its mirth,
Straightway my vision fills with blossoming
  Of summer sweets, and fragrant is the earth,
Meadows and lawns grow green; the wandering breeze
A tuneful troubadour among the trees.
  Sings softly, wooing beauty into birth,
Birds carol, children shout, and earth and sky
Blend like the notes of perfect harmony.

THE UNIVERSAL ROBBER.

IME, thy cunning thefts I trace,
In the mirror of my face.
In what hour of sleep did'st thou
Pluck the brown hair from my pow,
And, with fingers deft and sly,
Steal bright laughter from mine eye:
Charm away the careless quip
From the sumach-blooded lip.
And, grown bold, from soft hands press,
Radiant warmth and nimbleness,
And so changing the fair show
That myself I scarcely know?

THE REFORMER.

HE streams that feed the thirsty land,
    Give largess freely as they flow,
From mountain rivulets expand
    And, strong-armed, sweep the vales below;

And eddying on, through bay and bight,
    Through lonely wild and lovely lea,
By scarpéd cliff and stormy height,
    In mighty rivers reach the sea.

So shall he grow who gives to life
    High purposes and lofty deeds,
Who sees the calm above the strife
    Of blinded self and narrow creeds.

Oh, large of heart! oh, nobly great!
    He scorns the thrall of sect and clan,
Shakes off the fetters forged in hate,
    And claims a brotherhood with man.

Dwarfed Ignorance fills the world with wail,
    Opinion sneers at his advance;
And Error, rusted in his mail,
    Strides forth to meet him, lance to lance.

Mean, pigmy souls that cringe to form
    And fatten on the dregs of time,
Start from the dust in their alarm,
    And prate of rashness, treason, crime.

Law's wrinkled, cunning advocates
    Quote mummied precedents and rules,
The relics of barbaric states,
    The maxims of med'eval schools.

For him the tyrant's guard is set,
    For him the bigot's fagots fired,
For him the headsman's ax is whet,
    And chains are forged and minions hired.

Strong in his purpose, patient still,
    He wrestles with the doubts of mind,
And shakes the iron thews of will,
    As oaks are shaken by the wind.

Invincible in God and Truth,
    To smite the errors of his age
He gives the fiery force of youth,
    The tempered wisdom of the sage.

He sees, as prophets saw afar,
    In faith and vision wrapped sublime,
The coming of the Morning Star,
    The glory of the latter time.

His faith, outreaching circumstance,
    Beholds, beyond the narrow range
Of present time, the slow advance
    Of cycles bringing wondrous change.

He hears the mighty march of mind,
    The stately steppings of the free,
Where glorious in the sun and wind,
    Their blazoned banners yet shall be.

Well can he wait: the seed that lies
    Hid in the cold, repulsive clay,
Shall burst in after centuries,
    And spread its glories to the day.

Well can he wait: though sown in tears
    And martyred blood, with scourge and stripe,
God watches through the whirling years,
    And quickens when the hour is ripe.

Man's hands may fail, the slackened rein
    Drop from his nerveless grasp, but still
The wheels shall thunder on the plain,
    Rolled by the lightning of his will.

FORT DU QUESNE:

A HISTORICAL CENTENNIAL BALLAD.

November 25, 1758—1858.

I.

OME, fill the beaker, while we chaunt a pean of old days:
By Mars! no men shall live again more worthy of our praise,
Than they who stormed at Louisburg and Frontenac amain,
And shook the English standard out o'er the ruins of Du Quesne.

For glorious were the days they came, the soldiers strong and true,
And glorious were the days, they came for Pennsylvania, too;
When marched the troopers sternly on through forest's autumn brown,
And where St. George's cross was raised, the oriflamme went down.

Virginia sent her chivalry and Maryland her brave,
And Pennsylvania to the cause her noblest yeomen gave:
O, and proud were they who wore the garb of Indian hunters then,
For every sturdy youth was worth a score of common men!

They came from Carolina's pines, from fruitful Delaware—
The staunchest and the stoutest of the chivalrous were there;
And calm and tall above them all, i' the red November sun,
Like Saul above his brethren, rode Colonel Washington.

O'er leagues of wild and waste they passed, they forded stream and fen,
Where danger lurked in every glade, and death in every glen;
They heard the Indian ranger's cry, the Frenchman's far-off hail,
From purple distance echoed back through the hollows of the vale.

And ever and anon they came, along their dangerous way,
Where, ghastly, 'mid the yellow leaves, their slaughtered comrades lay;
The tartans of Grant's Highlanders were sodden yet and red,
As routed in the rash assault they perished as they fled.

—Ah! many a lass ayont the Tweed shall rue the fatal fray,
And high Virginian dames shall mourn the ruin of that day,
When gallant lad and cavalier i' the wilderness were slain,
'Twixt laureled Loyalhanna and the outposts of Du Quesne.

And there before them was the field of massacre and blood,
Of panic, rout and shameful flight, in that disastrous wood
Where Halket fell and Braddock died, with many a noble one
Whose white bones glistened through the leaves i' the pale November sun.

Then spoke the men of Braddock's Field, and hung their heads in shame,
For England's tarnished honor and for England's sullied fame;
"And, by St. George!" the soldiers swore, "we'll wipe away the stain
Before to-morrow's sun-set, at the trenches of Du Quesne."

II.

'Twas night along the autumn hills, the sun's November gleam
Had left its crimson on the leaves, its tinge upon the stream;
And Hermit Silence kept his watch 'mid ancient rocks and trees,
And placed his finger on the lip of babbling brook and breeze.

The bivouac's set by Turtle Creek: and while the soldiers sleep,
The swarthy chiefs around their fires an anxious council keep.
Some spoke of murmurs in the camp, scarce whispered to the air,
But tokens of discouragement, the presage of despair.

Some a retreat advised; 'twas late; the winter drawing on;
The forage and provision, too—so Ormsby said—were gone
Men could not feed on air and fight: whatever Pitt might say.
In praise or censure, still, they thought, 'twere wiser to delay.

Then up spoke iron-headed Forbes, and through his feeble frame
There ran the lightning of a will that put them all to shame:
"I'll hear no more," he roundly swore; "we'll storm the fort amain!
I'll sleep in h—l to-morrow night, or sleep in Fort Du Quesne!"

So said: and each to sleep addressed his wearied limbs and mind,
And all was hushed i' the forest, save the sobbing of the wind,
And the tramp, tramp, tramp of the sentinel, who started oft in fright
At the shadows wrought 'mid the giant trees by the fitful camp-fire light.

Good Lord! what sudden glare is that that reddens all the sky,
As though hell's legions rode the air and tossed their torches high!
Up, men! the alarm drum beats to arms! and the solid ground seems riven
By the shock of warring thunderbolts in the lurid depth of heaven!

O there was clattering of steel, and mustering in array,
And shouts and wild huzzas of men, impatient of delay,
As came the scouts swift-footed in—"They fly! the foe! they fly!
They've fired the powder magazine and blown it to the sky!"

III.

Now morning o'er the frosty hills in autumn splendor came,
And touched the rolling mists with gold, and flecked the clouds with flame:
And through the brown woods on the hills—those altars of the world—
The blue smoke from the settler's hut and Indian's wigwam curled.

Yet never, here, had morning dawned on such a glorious din
Of twanging trump, and rattling drum, and clanging culverin,
And glittering arms and sabre gleams and serried ranks of men,
Who marched with banners high advanced along the river glen.

O, and royally they bore themselves who knew that o'er the seas
Would speed the glorious tidings from the loyal Colonies,
Of the fall of French dominion with the fall of Fort Du Quesne,
And the triumph of the English arms from Erie to Champlain.

Before high noon they halted; and while they stood at rest,
They saw, unfolded gloriously the "Gateway of the West,"
There flashed the Allegheny, like a scimetar of gold,
And king-like in its majesty, Monongahela rolled:

Beyond, the River Beautiful swept down the woody vales,
Where Commerce, ere a century passed, should spread her thousand sails;
Between the hazy hills they saw Contrecœur's armed batteaux,
And the flying, flashing, feathery oars of the Ottawas' canoes.

Then, on from rank to rank of men, a shout of triumph ran,
And while the cannon thundered, the leader of the van,
The tall Virginian, mounted on the walls that smouldered yet,
And shook the English standard out, and named the place Fort Pitt.

Again with wild huzzas the hills and river valleys ring,
And they swing their loyal caps in air, and shout—"Long live the King!
"Long life unto King George!" they cry, "and glorious be the reign
That adds to English statesmen Pitt, to English arms Du Quesne."

ODE.

1.

NE hundred years ago to-day,
    In martial state the heroes came,
    To plant within the wilderness
      Their grand old English name and fame.
    They saw the glory of the land,
    The realm of nations yet to be,
And wrested from the allied foe
    The Empire of the Free.

United thus may Saxon sires
  And sons forever face the foe,
And strike for Freedom as they struck
  One hundred years ago.

II.

One hundred years have passed—and Peace
  In golden fullness o'er us reigns,
Full Plenty smiles on all our hills,
  And Gladness sings in all our plains.
The flag of freemen greets the air
  Where waved the standard of our sires,
And all their altars still are bright
  With Freedom's sacred fires.
    Here Fame shall keep in holy trust
      The names of those who met the foe,
    And won for us this glorious land
      One hundred years ago.

III.

So aid us, Heaven, to keep our trust,
  That in the coming centuries,
They'll say, Where truth and valor live
  The light of Freedom never dies.
God of our fathers! keep us still
  The chosen people of Thy hand,
One in our fealty to Thee,
  One to our native land.
    O guide us, while we watch and guard,
      From inward strife and outward foe,
    The heritage so nobly won
      One hundred years ago.

PITTSBURG.

EILED in thick clouds, shut in by shelving hills,
    The city of a thousand forges lies,
    Nor feels the pleasant glow of sunny skies.
    Hard toil have they who, in her thundering mills,
    Stir the white-heated metal or draw out
  The lengthening bar, or at the ponderous wheel
  Turn the huge shaft and shape the edging steel.
How like a hell from pit and chimney spout
The tumbling smoke and lapping flames that light
    The sky like torches, and reflecting quiver
    Along the tremulous surface of the river.
Unlovely though she be, in Freedom's might
Her strong hands build—buttress and tower and crest—
    The iron gate-way to the golden West.

A SONNET.

SO delicate and fair! to me thou art
  A semblance of the frailest, tenderest thing
  That blooms on earth or sports on silken wing.
Child of the skies, of Heaven the purest part,
Yet all of woman in thy loving heart!
  Thou cam'st to us when the mild airs of spring
  Blew open the first flowers; when first birds sing
In the fresh-budding forests thou'lt depart
Like them, I fear, when life's declining year
  Brings the rough winds and pitiless storms, that fly
  Like angry fiends across the sullen sky.
And the dark days,—dull, desolate and drear.
Who then shall answer to my heart's lone sigh?
Or who regret the loss when sick of life I die?

MOUNT GILBO.

SHOULDST thou e'er visit Mount Gilbo,
Fail not at early morn to go,
When the crimson Orient spreads a glow
O'er the mountain's ancient robe of snow;
When flash the long, swift lines of light
Into the valleys that clasp the night,
And the mists that cover glen and wold
Roll off like a sea of molten gold.

High is the peak of Mount Gilbo,
Robed in a thousand winters' snow,
Jagged and forked its massive rocks,
Rent by lightning and thunder shocks—
Scathed by the tempest's glance of light
Rushing by on the wings of night;
Deep are the gorges on its sides,
Fearful the chasms where gloom abides,
Where torrents roar and boil and hiss,
Down in the fathomless, black abyss.

Beautiful glaciers on Mount Gilbo!
Beautiful, ay, when the sun's first glow
Touches their domes and their crystal spires,
Lighting them up with a thousand fires;
Weaving the many hues that form
The iris-arch on the flying storm
Into some rare and rich device,
In each atom of lucent ice.

Not the irradiate halls that lie
Far from the ken of mortal eye,
Down in the green depths of the sea,
Can by half so radiant be,
Though they be flooded with fairy light,
Mystical, glorious, dazzling, bright.
Ever changing, but always fair,
Shaping to something quaint and rare,
Now a mosque, with minarets
Tipt and blazoned with jasper sets,
Now a temple, lofty and old,
Fretted with amethyst and gold,
Again, a forest of burnished spears,
Brighter as clearer the sun appears,
Whose scintillant tips like brilliants show
Over the frozen hills of snow.
Thus do the glaciers of Mount Gilbo,
Sparkle and shimmer and flash and glow,
Till they seem to change in the broad sun's glare
To phantasies in the frosty air.

Solemn the night that gathers round
Those icy heights in the vast profound,
When the stars look out from pure blue skies,
Clearer, brighter and larger in size,
Down on the peak of old Gilbo,
Sternly bold in his robe of snow.
Silently cuts the raven's wing
   Through the cold, cold mountain air,
As though fearing the Tempest King,
   Who brews the storm and hurricane there.
In the forest far below,
From hoar oaks green with mistletoe,
Hoots the owl and caws the crow,

And the wail of the woods is long and deep,
As the winds through countless branches sweep,
Tossing the tall tops to and fro,
Very majestically and slow,
Like the plumes of a craped and bannered train,
  When hearts beat sad for the mighty gone,
And feet are heavy that would remain
    Where greatness sleeps in the dust alone.

Dismal the night when the tempest whines,
Through the boughs of the stunted pines,
When ominous voices call aloud
From caverned rock and sable cloud,
And the fires of heaven glance and leap
From crag to crag, and from steep to steep,
And the solid walls of granite rock,
As rent by an earthquake's rumbling shock:
Then the demons of mountain gloom
Issue forth from each cavern-tomb,
And horrible shapes and phantoms fly
  On the ragged folds of the raven clouds,
And ghouls and gnomes go gibbering by,
  And the ghosts of the wicked walk in shrouds.
O God! 'tis a fearful thing to stay
  Where the avalanche hurls its bolts of snow,
And thunders sound a reveille
  Amid the passes of Mount Gilbo.

THE HERMIT OF MOUNT GILBO,

AND THE ANGEL CONVOY, CHRISTMAS NIGHT.

HE snows came down on the mountain brown,
White and soft as the cygnet's down;
The stunted pines on the shelving steeps
Bent with the pure and crystal heaps,
The winds were low, the torrents still,
The snows lay evenly on the hill,
And evening shades were coming down
    On valley dark and mountain brown.
The bells swang joyfully to and fro,
    Right jollily and merrily,
    Right laughingly and cheerily,
  In the belfry tower of the convent dim,
Down in the vale that lay below,
Under the shadow of Mount Gilbo,
    Where the nuns were chanting the Advent Hymn.
For it was Michælmas' joyful time,
The bells were ringing a lively chime,
When the snows and the evening shades came down
On the murky vale and the mountain brown.

In a cavern of Mount Gilbo
    Dwelt a hermit, a pious man,
    He was hight "good Hilde Ban;"
His gray beard down to his knees did flow,
    His long locks over his shoulders fell,
Whiter with eld than the mountain snow,
    But his eye was bright as a young gazelle's.

THE HERMIT OF MOUNT GILBO.

Who he was, or whence he came,
Of gentle blood or the child of shame,
None did know, but many a tale
Was told by the peasants in the vale,
Of the merciful deeds of Hilde Ban,
Who was deemed by all a marvelous man.
Many a year had he dwelt there;
His food was the scantiest, coarsest fare,
And his drink, of the pure and crystal rill,
Leaping to light from the rocky hill.
His garb was coarse—a flowing coat,
Made from the hair of the mountain goat,
Spun and wove in its native hue,
A sort of mixture of gray and blue.
Deep in the gloom of his awful cell,
That suited his mournful ways right well,
Sat the hermit Christmas eve,
And heartily o'er his sins did grieve.
Then knelt he down on the cold, damp stone,
Very solemnly and alone—
Before Madonna's statue knelt,
   Muttered his "Avè" o'er and o'er,
   Bowed to the hard and flinty floor,
And through the darkness feebly felt
For the silent stone: and kissed the toe,
Saying his Aves slow and low,
While chattered his teeth with the bitter cold,
And blue were his features shrivelled and old;
Counted his beads with numb, thin hands,
Regularly as the sands
Through the hour-glass stilly fall,
Or the tick of a clock in an antique hall,
When the rooks in the dead night-watches call;
Clasped he them in his hands so cold,
So skeleton, bony, stiff and old,
And still his paternosters told.

Then lay him down on the rocks so bare,
Where swept the keen and nipping air,
Where crept the frosts that silently were
Busy, busy everywhere:
Clasped his crucifix in prayer:
Lay him down in his mountain cell,
And deep sleep on his spirit fell—
Jesu, Marie! shield him well!

In his vision he saw, and lo!
His cell with light was all aglow—
With spectral brilliancy aglow!
It shimmered and flashed on the frosty wall,
Brighter than shines in palace hall,
When high is the voice of festival;
And there was music unutterable:
The ear might hear—tongue can not tell
How soft on his ravished ear it fell.
He smiled—how sweet! in his raptured sleep,
His skeleton hands the measure keep;
And he laughed aloud, did Hilde Ban,
That grave and pious-hearted man!
He laughed aloud, he laughed for joy,
He was never so glad since when a boy!
The statue of Madonna shone,
With a glory from the Father's throne;
And by his side an angel stood,
And called him "Hilde Ban the good:"
He was clad in raiment like to gold,
Exceedingly beautiful to behold,
    And a crown of light was on his head;
His smile a great approval told
    Of the pious life the hermit led.
Much was Hilde Ban's surprise,
And he humbly veiled his dazzled eyes,

And he bowed to the presence from the skies.
His was holy awe and pious fear
As the angel cried, "What do'st thou here?
Lo! Hilde Ban, I have come for thee!
Thou hast suffered much, and hast borne it well,
In sorrow thou no more shalt dwell,
Thou'st been a brother to thy kind,
Hast served thy God with heart and mind,
    Come up with me, come up with me;"
And holy voices loudly cried,
And unseen voices on every side,
Through all the glorified air replied,
    "Come up with me, come up with me."

    *   *   *   *   *

At dapple dawn the following day,
A chamois hunter passed that way—
As merry a free-born mountaineer
As hunted the antelope and deer:
Joyously sang he his roundelay,
As he groped to the hermit's cell his way;
For he loved the anchorite old and gray,
And he brought him food; but when he found
The hermit stark on the flinty ground,
"God's sooth!" cried he, "he's in a swound!"
And a very long breath the hunter drew,
His brown, plump features softer grew,
And his eye-lids seemed to drop with dew,
As kindly he raised the old man's head,
And found that Hilde Ban was dead!
But nothing knew he of the glad, glad sight
    That the hermit saw but yester-even.
That made him laugh in his sleep outright,
When the angels came on Christmas night,
    And bore his pious soul to heaven.

A WOMAN'S TEAR.

THINK not that the strength of prayer
    Is breathed alone in words of flame,
The whirlwind might of eloquence
    When roused by conscious wrong is tame—
Is tame when measured by that power,
  Deep, silent, earnest and sincere,
Which melts the will as wax to flame,
  And voiceless pleads in woman's tear.

A POOR MAN'S THANKSGIVING.

LET him who eats not, think he eats,
   'Tis one to him who last year said,
"My neighbor dines on dainty sweets
   And I on coarser bread."

He who on sugar angels fares
   Hath pangs beneath his silken vest;
The rougher life hath fewer cares—
   Who fasts hath sounder rest.

If lean the body, light the wings;
   His fancy hath more verge and room,
Who feasts upon the wind that brings
   The flowers of hope to bloom.

So, if no smoking turkey grace
   This day my clean but humble board,
I'll think what might have been my case
   If rich, and thank the Lord.

No gout awaits my coming age,
   No bulbous nose like lobster red,
To vex my temper into rage,
   Or fill my days with dread.

Leave to the rich his roast and wine;
   Death waits on him who waits for all;
The doctor will be there by nine,
   By twelve the priest will call.

Lord, in all wholesome, moderate ways
   Keep me, lest it should hap me worse;
Teach one to fill his mouth with praise
   Who never filled his purse.

EN MEMOIRE.

(Amelia B. Welby.)

CLOSE the dim eyes with tenderness—her rest
Is as an infant's, knowing naught of care;
Fold the cold arms upon her lily breast;
'Tis well—'tis well: lay back the long, dark hair,
And place a rose in its first blushes there.
'Tis well—'Tis well: she loved a rose in bloom,
And life near death looks beautiful and fair—
There seems a spirit in that rose perfume
That, like unchanging love, survives beyond the tomb.

Smooth down the pillow softly—so—'tis well,
And tenderly compose her form to sleep;
Look now—how beautiful! ye can not tell
In words the sorrow that in tears ye weep.
Once more—it is the last fond look!—how deep,
How strong the utterance for the loss you moan!

EN MEMOIRE.

    All's over now!—no more you'll need to keep
    The watch of love and pity; she is gone
Forever from your sight, and oh, your heart how lone!

    But yesterday, and like the rising lark
    She caroled in the glory of her song;
    Before the coming on of eve, how dark
    Death's solemn messengers around her throng!
    You saw the shadows that to graves belong
    Dim the clear lustre of her peaceful eyes;
    You saw the red hue come and go, and long
    You hoped, until, unloosed life's tender ties,
She died, as music's strain in the far echo dies.

    For her I weep, though stranger to her thought
    And to her presence, yet to me her strain
    Was an unsullied pleasure, overwrought
    Sometimes by joy's intensity to pain;
    And though to her my tears are as the rain
    Upon the sterile desert to the rose
    The bulbul sings to — useless, idle, vain —
    Yet must I weep; for not the least of woes,
To one who loves a song, is its eternal close.

    Weave me a garland of the asphodel,
    The dark-leaved cypress and the mournful yew,
    Bring hither locust boughs from yonder dell,
    Wall-flowers of scarlet, night-shades palely blue,
    And grave-grown myrtle weeping wet with dew.
    They do accord with mournfulness, and bear
    A sympathy to sorrow, and renew
    The hope of happiness, and breathe a prayer
For those who from our sight have gone where angels are.

Wail low, ye winds; babble, thou thoughtless stream
To the rose bending o'er thee — what to me
Or mine art thou? Swift as thy flow the stream
Of life sweeps onward to eternity.
A moment, and we are no more to be;
No record of our names, no tongue to tell
That here I wandered weeping near by thee,
And bowed my spirit to a stroke that fell
Upon that better one whose being was a spell.

A spell of song; ay, such a spell as charmed
All passionate ears in Arqua's quiet vale;
Or in thy Tuscan lays, Bocaccio, warmed
The magic fervency of many a tale;
Or in St. Anna's prison did prevail
O'er a heart eat with sorrow, till the night
Of the long solitude began to fail
In the clear flame of Tasso's fancy's flight,
Which round those prison walls still sheds a hallowed light.

Simple and graceful was thy easy lay,
And unpremeditated as the lark's clear note,
When morning purples on the hill-tops grey.
Around us still their mingled echoes float
With a remembered gladness; and remote,
In other lands, where'er the Saxon tongue
Makes itself music, shall the strain thou'st wrote
Charm all whose hearts to beauty thrill or long
For inborn melody that shapes itself to song.

But these, thy groves, thy native hills and vales,
Where thou, their minstrel, hast enchanted long,
Shall hallowed be—thy spirit here prevails!
Like St. Cecelia, thou didst come in song,
And hast departed with it, and no wrong
Hath marred its sweetness; thou wilt be confessed,
Life's true interpreter, by many a tongue
In after years, when we forgotten rest—
AMELIA of our hearts, sweet songstress of the West.

OUR COUNTRY'S FLAG.

ET faction assail or oppression invade,
   Let treachery threaten or intrigue divide,
'Neath that banner will freemen draw swiftly the blade,
   And sweep back the foe as weeds swept by the tide.
Wherever those stars shall bespangle the sky
   There will freemen be found to defend them, or die!
      Shine stars of the Union!
        Wave flag of the free!
      The hope of the nations
        Is centered in thee!
We swear to defend, by the souls of the brave,
It's honor, wherever that banner shall wave.

Are the stars on our banner less brilliant to-day,
   Than when, in the hour of their trial and gloom,
The heroes we honor they led to the fray,
   To conquer for freedom or hallow her tomb?
Do we love them the less, as they glitter afar,
Our herald in peace and our standard in war?
      By the deeds of the valiant,
        The blood of the slain,
      By the rights that we cherish,
        The cause we maintain.
Their honor we swear, by the souls of the brave,
To guard well wherever our banner shall wave!

LOVE'S HERALDS.

LOVE'S Mercuries are invisible; they come
    And sing, like Ariel, in the enchanted air,
  While we with wonder and delight sit dumb,
  Not knowing how it is, nor whence, nor where;
And they, like swans that rest on billowy seas,
    Glide on the gently pulsing melodies,
While we start—listen—cry in glad surprise
    "'Tis here!" and the next moment Echo cries, "'tis there!"

HEAVEN'S EVANGELS.

THE tenderest flower the soonest dies,
   The sweetest strain seems soonest ended;
   The beautiful but tempts our eyes,
Then, still enticing, mounts the skies,
   And with the world unseen is blended.

And so the gifts we most approve,
   From heaven sent down, to us are given
To link our hearts to them in love,
Which done, they pass from earth above,
   And, thus our hearts are drawn to heaven.

OSSIAN TO HIS HARP.

FAREWELL my harp! In Cona's vale
   Thy trembling strings shall wake no more;
The master's skillful fingers fail,
   The minstrel's song is o'er.
Wild harp of Selma, to thy tone
   No more shall valiant bosoms thrill,
Nor beauty's sighs thy passion own—
   Neglected—broken—still.

In Lutha's vale the bard will sleep
   Near rocks where purple thistles bloom,
And heroes' shades their vigils keep
   Around the minstrel's tomb.
But thou divinest! who shall call
   The spirit from thy slumbering strings,
When o'er thy master's bier the pall
   Its mournful sable flings?

Companion of my song, thy strain
   To deeds of glory called the brave,
Or wailed when on the martial plain
   Was heaped the warriors' grave.
Round thee, enchanter! ne'er again
   Shall Morven's chieftains throng;
And Selma's maids will seek in vain
   The magic of my song.

OSSIAN TO HIS HARP.

Alas! my days of song are o'er;
    The sword hangs idle on the wall,
The voice of Cona sounds no more
    In Fingal's silent hall.
By Mora's rock my step shall fail,*
    To heather flowers my head be press'd,
Nor can the rude and sounding gale
    Disturb the minstrel's rest.

Hung on the oak by Mora's stone,
    In mournful muteness thou'lt deplore
The Car-borne Fingal's mighty son, †
    The bard, whose song is o'er;
Then, harp of Selma, thou wilt tell
    The winds that oft thy strings shall try,
The minstrel's spirit still doth dwell
    In every broken sigh.

The noble chiefs of future years
    Shall hear, sweet harp, thy growing fame,
And beauty's fairest lips, with tears
    Repeat the minstrel's name.
Wild harp of Selma, though thy strings
    Neglected and forgotten lie,
The spirit of thy song still sings
    In every broken sigh.

---

* By the stone of Mora I shall fall asleep.
† The hunter shall come forth in the morning, and the voice of my harp shall be heard no more, "Where is the son of Car-borne Fingal?" and the tear shall be on his cheek.—*Ossian*.

TELL ME TRUE.

I.

Now the springing grasses spread
    In the pastures where the flags and willows grow,
For the tender lambs a bed;
    And the bob-o-links are there,
    Waking into song the air
Of the valley in the sunlight all aglow.

II.

There dainty sweets must be
    The pale anemone,
There buttercups and crocus tinct with gold
    And roses, wild and rare,
    In the music breathing air
Blush with secrets love in whispers there has told.

III.

O, children tell me true,
Are the skies as bright to you,
And the wimple of the brook as soft and low,
As when I, without a care,
Gathered early cowslips there
In the splendor of the morning long ago?

IV.

Then lead me by the hand,
O'er the pleasant, pleasant land,
Through orchards fair and meadows let us go;
But the hearts that beat with mine
In the days that seemed divine,
O, ye dearlings of my soul, ye can not know.

THE HERO OF THE ARCTIC.

"Stuart Hollins could not be induced to leave the ship; his post was at the guns from first to last, giving signals; he kept firing at intervals, till the ship went down. We saw him in the very act of firing as the vessel disappeared under the water."— *Tobin's Statement.*

I.

ON the quarter deck of the Arctic stood
   The hero boy, undaunted,
Like Faith with her calm heart unsubdued,
   And her angel face enchanted,
While stout hearts quailed and wildly rose
   The tempest of commotion,
The brave boy gave the signal guns
   To the misty waste of ocean.

II.

Despair and the phantom terrors round
   The masts and spars are flying,
While wildly sweep o'er the surging waves
   The shrieks of the lost and dying.
But hark! though the death pall hangs above
   And the grave is yawning under,
The signal gun through the misty gloom
   Still speaks in tones of thunder.

III.

Then the craven fled, and the timid wept,
   And prayers to heaven were given,
As the foaming waters round them closed,
   And the iron ribs were riven.

But lo! the dun clouds glow and glare—
  The masts are wildly reeling,
The signal blaze the calm pale form
  Of the hero boy revealing.

IV.

Slow sinks the gallant ship; the sea
  Her green waves o'er her meeting;
And the hearts that thrilled to love and fear
  Forgot the woe of beating.
But hark! the signal gun once more!—
  And the clouds repeat the story—
Brave boy! that halo light to death
  Was thy halo light to glory.

WHY MOURN, O FRIEND?

HY mourn, O friend, or grief-grown fillets wear?
    Since those we love have fallen by the way,
For them no more life's weary round of care,
    Its nights of sorrow, or its strifes by day.

The morn saw one depart, and one the eve,
  But ere they faded from our sorrowing view,
Saw ye not from their eyes death's shadow leave,
And Beulah's nightless glories beaming through.

STAR OF THE EVENING

STAR of the evening,
  Glory on high,
Queen of the beautiful
  Gem of the sky,
Light of the traveler
  Seeking for rest,
Ever thus peacefully
  Look from the west.

Eyes that are watching
  Gaze upon thee—
Eyes that are weary
  Waiting for me;
Joy of the wanderer,
  Evermore shine,
Smiling I gaze on thee—
  Smile thou on mine.

MAKE IT FOUR, YER HONOR.

AS ye iver in coort av a mornin'
   Whin the shiverin' craythers come
Like bastes, from their iron cages,
   To be tould their guilt an' doom?
Some av thim bould an' brazen,
   Some av thim broke wid care,
Some av them wildly wapin',
   Or sullen wid black despair.

O it's a sight inthirely
   To take the heart away!
The pitiful little childer,
   The ould ones dirthy an grey—
Crouchin' along the binches,
   Tuckin' their rags about
To hide the sorrow that's in thim,
   And kape the couldness out.

The Joodge sits up above thim,
   The coort's own officers;
Polace wid their long shillalys,
   Nate in their coats and stars;
Witnisses, too, a plinty;
   Shysters to worry an' bite;
And hangin' about the railin'
   The divil's own crew for fight.

Nine av the clock is sthrikin'
 Whin the clerk begins to rade,
And prisintly his Honor
 Says to the coort "Procade."
Thin up they call ould Mary;
 An' trimblin' there she stands—
The combs forgotten that smoothed her hair,
 And the soap that scoured her hands.

.........Larry, my boy, where are ye
 That came from ould Galway,
An' brought in yer arms a darlin',
 The swatest that crossed the say?
There wasn't the likes for beauty
 By silver Shannon set
Since the sun first shone in heaven,
 And the grass wid dew was wet.

Could ye see her now, all faded,
 In her rags, an' sin, an' shame,
Your heart it would break wid sorrow
 For the girl that bore your name;
Yer heart it would break for thinkin'
 Av the proud day ye was wed—
Ah! better the silence av the grave,
 And the darkness av the dead.........

Thin up spakes the Joodge, an' says he,
 "Mary, ye've been here
How many times, can ye tell me,
 Since it was the last New Year?
Ye're scarcely quit av the prisin,
 And here ye are to-day
For sthalin', says the witness:
 Now what have ye to say?"

MAKE IT FOUR, YER HONOR.

Shakin' her grey hairs backward
  Out of her eyes and face:
"It's thrue that ye say, yer Honer.
  It's thrue is my disgrace.
It wasn't the coat I cared for;
  It's stharvin I was to ate,
And I want a friendly shilter
  Out av a friendless sthrate.

"Sind me back to the prisin,
  For the winter it is could,
An' there isn't a heart that's warmin'
  For the likes av me that's ould;
There isn't a heart that's warmin',
  Nor a hand that takes me in—
If I sthale to kape from stharvin'
  May God forgive the sin!"

Then kindly spakes his Honer:
  "Well, Mary, will it do
If I sind ye to the prisin
  For jist a month or two?"
"The prisin's a friend," says Mary:
  "I fear the winter more—
An it's all the same, yer Honer,
  Ye'll plaze to make it four."

THE BROWN CHICKADEE.

A FABLE.

IN the top of an oak sat a brown chickadee;
It seemed but a speck for the height of the tree;
And it chirruped and twittered, till straightway it saw
Through the green leaves the forms of a dove and a daw.
Then it fluttered its wings, and it puffed out its breast,
And the feathers stood up from its tail to its crest—
"The impertinent jades!" in its anger it cried,
"Do they think that with them this fine tree I'll divide?
They shall see I know how to resent, though I'm small,
And a tree good for one will not do for us all."
So he hopped from his perch, did the brown chickadee,
And left them alone on a limb of the tree—
All unconscious the dove, and my story grows sad,
For the daw never dreamed that the titmouse was mad!

MORAL.

If angered by what others do, and would show it,
Be sure that you act so the others will know it.

THE TWO MARINERS.

COLUMBUS gave a world to light;
    Found tropic isles in tropic seas,
    Where spicewinds, wafting melodies
    From gorgeous groves of orange trees,
Thrilled the pleased senses with delight.
Nor sooner he these prizes gains
Than ingrates send him back in chains.

In thee, sweet one, my venturous heart—
    A mariner o'er untried seas—
    Found isles of calm and joy and ease,
    More glorious than the Cyclades—
New words in which it claimed a part;
Yet thence, where such enchantment reigns,
Thou'st sent the wanderer back in chains.

THE EMIGRANT'S INVITATION.

WILL you come to the land where the song of the lark
Is heard in the woodland from morning till dark;
Where the violets open their tender blue eyes
To the zephyrs of spring and the warmth of the skies;
Where the prairies are laden with honey-lipped flowers,
More fragrant than blossom in Ottoman bowers?
    Will you come to that Land?
Then with me, love, away, like a bird to its nest,
To the empire of freedom, the West, ho! the West!

There the hunter his carol awakens at dawn,
And the blast of his bugle arouses the fawn,
While the clattering hoof, and the echoing gun,
Announce to his comrades, the chase is begun!
Ho! to sweep like the wild horse the dew-beaded plain,
With a heart like your swift steed, uncurbed by a rein.
    Will you come to that Land?
Then with me, love, away, like a bird to its nest,
To the home of the free in the West, ho! the West!

'Tis a land of broad empires, whose bounds shall enfold
Full seedtimes of promise, rich harvests of gold,
Where from valley to mountain, from river to sea,
Shall ascend the hosannas, the songs of the free;
Where the exiles of nations, the children of toil,
Shall be lords of themselves and the kings of the soil!
    Will you come to that Land?
Then away, love, away, where the sun sinks to rest,
O'er the empire of freemen, the West, ho! the West!

FROM THEIR SERENE ABODES.

ROM their serene abodes how calm and still
    The everlasting stars look down,
So shone they on Judea's sacred hill
    Ere Israel's royal minstrel wore the crown.

There flames Arcturus, and Orion there
    And Ariadne on her milky throne
As when from Belas' height the Coptic seer
    Proclaimed thy destiny, O Babylon!

Through the gigantic ages, as with spears
    Tipt with quick beams of unextinguished light,
Far reaching they, through all the circling years
    Have smote the mantle of chaotic night.

The wise, the good, the manly and the fair—
    Youth fresh in life, and age its vigor o'er—
Have gazed upon thee shining ever there—
    Have gazed and vanished, to return no more.

Each with his little world of hope and fears,
    His dear ambitions and his favorite schemes,
Hath wrought expectant through the round of years,
    And passed to rest within the land of dreams.

A gentle slumber falling like the air,
    When twilight shades the dewy valleys keep,
Hath passed on all, and sweetly wooed from care,
    To lap the weary in the arms of sleep.

There in the vale, or yonder on the plain,
　They laid aside their cares o'er those to weep
Who, gone before, had rent time's veil in twain,
　Then all their woes forgot, themselves to sleep.

So pilgrims struggling o'er some storm-vexed height
　To sunny vales their heavy steps incline,
Pause at the base, where slumbrous airs invite,
　Fold their tired arms, and all their toils resign.

THE MORNING PRAYER.

THESE rusty steel spectacles—there is the case—
Bring back to my mind a much faded old face,
And the Elder once more, seated solemnly there,
Makes ready to sanctify breakfast with prayer.

How fresh is the landscape, how cool and how still,
With shade in the valley and sun on the hill,
The cattle in pasture, the sheep near the fold,
And meadows with buttercups blazing like gold.

Through the rose-latticed window that looks to the east,
The sunbeams dance brightly like lambs at a feast,
And flash from old pewters that came o'er the sea,
Ere Boston rose up against tyrants and tea.

What fragrance the glowing tin coffee-pot spreads,
As it simmers and sings to us snug in our beds,
While the boiling potatoes bump round in the pot,
And the pan of brown biscuits stands ready and hot.

There's Tab on the hearth rug, and Tray at the door,
Keeping watch lest the chickens come tracking the floor,
While Aunty the anxious, makes vocal the air,
To hasten us children to breakfast and prayer.

Dear Aunt! can I ever forget that rare shelf
With its candlesticks, snuffers, blue china and delf,
Dried peppermint, saffron, sage, senna and squills,
All ready to conquer colds, colics and chills!

No wonder thy kind face grew withered and thin
Thinking how we might perish in childhood and sin,
For there stood the apple-tree close by the wall
To tempt us like Adam to eat and to fall.

At last we are ready; two chubby-cheeked boys
Most happy when raising a whirlwind of noise;
Two girls in whose eyes is the glow of the sun
As they brighten with laughter and sparkle with fun.

Now seated and still on our chip-bottomed chairs,
The Elder invites us to join him in prayers,
And reading a portion of Scripture, we kneel,
While he pours out his soul in a fervent appeal.

Then up we glance softly, two boys russet brown,
And sisters as fair as a peach in its down.
With a grace like a saint's in its sweetest repose
With dimples as deep as the heart of a rose.

* * * * *

PHILO IS DEAD.

PHILO is dead! the gay, the gentle boy—
The valley's glory—Philo is no more.
Of limb elastic as the tempered bow,
He bounded o'er the hills, when first the sun
Shot crimson arrows up the flecking east:
From sweetly clovered steeps, kissed by first dews,
He called up airiest echoes from dusk vales,
Where yet the sturdy ox and lactant kine
Herded and dozed beside the gnarled oaks.
Those hills shall see him never, never more;
The cliffs that answered to his merry call
Bare their brown fronts in silence to the winds
That round them grieve and whisper sighing low.

Spring brings return of beauty; to the woods
Buds, leaves, and lichens tender; to the vale
Flowers, wandering vines, and verdure thickly strewn,
To the brier the rose, and to the thorn the flower;
To earth in all her recesses of light and shade,
The joy of sunshine and the mellow rain.
But not to me can she restore the joy
That with her presence faded: on his brow
Shone like a star the effluence of life
That made more radiant than the sun, than birds
More musical, than flowers more fair,
The wintriest gloom, or day tempestuous.
Listless I wander through the paths he trod:
There is the mossy knoll that oft received
The precious burden; there the tree he nursed,
Yonder the rose he tended, and its buds plucked off
In playful mood, so daintily to tip
The dancing tendrils of his golden hair.

Wrap me, O memory, in dreams; dissolve
In visions all that lies so dark between
The idle present and the happy past.
Feed me of old delights, O, fancy! fill
Each avenue of sense with nectared bliss
That time has hoarded from my heart bereft,
And like the witch of Endor, call thou up
Him round whose brow the rainbow of my hope
O'erarched the coming years so radiantly.
I watch—I call—"Philo!" the bosky dells
Echo and oft repeat the name—the hills
In lingering sweetness answer and reply.
Alas! he comes not. "Wherefore thus deceive
Thy heart," says Reason, "only to make sharp
The cruel griefs that sting afresh thy love?"
Will he not answer then? shall I no more
In shady nooks and sunny dells espy
The vision of his beauty? Here oft his feet,
White as the lilies in the dimpled lake,
Shook from the bells of golden throated flowers,
The purest pearls that ever night fays dropt
From tinted shells in aromatic cups,
Or like an alabaster peeped from out
The fresh green grass and pensive violet.
Ah! when the spring shall blush in all the vales
And dandelions star the hills with gold;
When in the coverts and the budding dells,
The fiery wild rose and the star flower blue,
The fragrant pea and crocus laid with gold,
Shall blossom and grow pale, he will return
In all the years no more. Philo is dead!
O, mourn, deserted hills, mourn Philo dead!
O, mourn, untrodden paths, mourn Philo dead!
O, mourn, unvocal vales, mourn Philo dead!

HER RECORD.

OW she is gone, most gentle of her kind,
    The lesson of her life who reads, may still
    Learn of the triumphs of th' impelling will,
The victories of the unconquerable mind
    Over the weakness of much human ill.
For so it was, though fragile as a flower,
You might discern the unbaffled spirit's power,
    Warding the blows that lesser natures kill.
The days she numbered by the deeds each hour
    Completed saw; and through her busy hands
    There slept no atom of time's sliding sands
Unused. Wife, mother, friend! thro' sun and shower,
    She plucked from many hearts the thorns of care,
    And left the rose of peace to blossom there.

SLEIGH-RIDE SONG.

MERRILY ho! away we go,
Over the fields of frozen snow,
Lightly we laugh, and lightly we sing,
   For Winter is jolly, and Winter is king.
      Then ho, ho, ho! then ha, ha, ha!
Leave sober faces to churls, heigh, ho!
   Was ever delight
   Like a frosty night,
And a sleigh full of laughing girls, heigh ho!

Merrily ho! how fleet we go,
Swift as the reindeer over the snow,
Jingling bells may tinkle and ring,
For somebody's jolly, and somebody'll sing,
      Then ho, ho, ho! then ha, ha, ha!
Leave sober faces to churls, heigh, ho!
   There's no delight
   Like a frosty night,
And a sleigh full of laughing girls, heigh, ho!

WAITING.

> "And the grasshopper shall be a burden, and desire shall fail: because man goeth to his long home."

DEATH is better than life,
And sleep is sweeter than waking.
   Sweeter is sleep than conscious
   Linking of sorrow to sorrow,
Leaness of spirit to body,
The frame thereof sorely shaking,
   Smitten by pain to-day
   And shattered by grief to-morrow.

Of this alone are we certain:
The shroud is woven to wind us,
   The mattock and worm are eager,
   The hearse and the mourners waiting.
Matters it, then, what time
We go to the houses assigned us?
   Let us be ready to face
   Our fate without hesitating.

We might endure did we know
There were anything lasting or real
    In love or pleasure or fame,
    In fortune, dominion or glory;
They are but shadows of shadows,
The shapes of a splendid ideal,
    That shine in the light of romance,
    And live in the pages of story.

Death is better than life,
And sweeter is rest than sighing.
    Sweeter is rest than care
    And getting of gold with sorrow,
And wisdom that seemeth folly,
With death from the house-top crying,
    "That which is thine to-day
    Mine shall it be to-morrow."

Vex not our ears with babble
Of increase of years and of riches,
    Corn and oil for plenty,
    And wine for gladness red,
Fruits and the fatness of seasons:
A voice from the darkness preaches,
    "These are for the living,
    But ye are for the dead."

Vex not our thoughts with delights
Of treasure of gold and fair raiment,
    Lights like the light of the sun,
    In houses of dancers and singers,
Where love unto love makes answer,
And heart unto heart makes payment,
    Coinage of rose-red kisses
    And toyings of passionate fingers.

Death is better than life,
And sweeter is peace than striving.
    Sweeter the valley in shadow
    Than wind-blown hills in splendor.
We are weary of labor,
Weary of long contriving,
    The flesh faints under its burdens,
    The soul cries out, surrender.

Into our hearts there enter
Neither the lights of morning,
    Neither glad voices of spring time,
    Neither the heats of summer;
Only the shadows of evening,
Only sad voices of warning,
    Only the frosts of winter,
    That make numb senses num'er.

Out of our lives are taken
Hopes of impossible things:
    The noise of the praise of the people
    And triumphs for deeds that are done;
Wealth of the fields and the rivers
Wrought in the splendor of kings,
    And a name of all names to be spoken
    In lands of the snow and the sun.

Death is better than life,
The reaping of grain than the sowing.
    Sweeter the folding of hands
    Than strength and the labor before us.
Why should we toil as one
For whom fresh seasons are blowing,
    When the sands slip under our feet
    And the heavens darken o'er us?

One there is who builds,
And his building is not shaken,
    Neither by roar of tempests,
    Nor roll of the thunder of drums;
Only the trumpet of God
The dwellers therein shall waken,
    When the wrath of His wrath is kindled
    And the day of His judgment comes.

With the peace that is before
And the pain that is behind us,
    Knowing the folly of living,
    The sorrow that comes of waiting,
It can not matter how soon
We go to the houses assigned us,
    For we are ready to face
    Our fate without hesitating.

IN REMEMBRANCE.

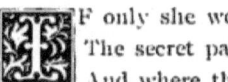

IF only she were here, who knew
    The secret paths of fields and woods,
And where the earliest wild flowers through
    Cool mosses push their dainty hoods;
Whose voice was like a mother's call
    To them, and bade them wake and rise,
And mark the morning's splendors fall
    In mists of pearl from tender skies:—

If only she were here, to see
    The landscape freshening hour by hour,
And watch in favorite plant and tree
    The bud unfold in leaf and flower;
To welcome back from sunny lands
    The bluebirds that have tarried long,
Or feed with her own loving hands
    The bright, red-breasted prince of song:—

If, brightening down th' accustomed walk,
    She came to welcome friend and guest,
To share our light, unstudied talk,
    And sparkle at the rising jest;
Or, leading on to nobler themes,
    In art and science play the sage,
And rapt, as in prophetic dreams,
    Foretell the wonders of the age:—

Could she return, as now the spring
    Returns in robes of green and gold,
When love and song are on the wing,
    And hearts forget that they are old—
How bright were all the days! how fair
    This miracle of life would be!
Whose pulsings thrill the glowing air
    And quicken over land and sea.

And shall we doubt thy presence here,
    Spirit of light, because our eyes,
Veiled in this earthly atmosphere,
    See not the heaven that near us lies?
More living thou than we, who stand
    Within the shadow of the years,
Whose glimpses of a better land
    Are caught through eyelids wet with tears—

And so in hope we wait, and see
    The springs return and summers go
That bring us nearer unto thee,
    Who art beside us, since we know
Whatever range thy flight may take,
    Its steps thou surely wilt retrace—
Love binds with cords death can not break,
    And draws thee from the realms of space!

SPIRITUS SYLVAE.

*Immortalia ne speres, monet annus, et almum
Quæ rapit hora diem.—Horace.*

*Nature finds tongues in trees, books in the running brooks,
Sermons in stones, and good in every thing.—Shaks.*

THERE are invisible spirits in the air!
They walk the earth with us, and minister,
In our communion with the visible,
To our immortal utterance. In the mute,
Impressive language of the natural world—
In flower and leaf, and in the flow of streams,
In the deep shadows of primeval groves,
In the eternal silence of the hills,
In change of seasons, and the flight of years.
They speak in eloquence to our inner sense
Of a mysterious Destiny, that rules,
Directs, decrees and stamps material forms,
And grosser being with the seal of death;
Yet, out of desolation shadows forth
The glorious meaning of that principle,
Which gives to life desire, and longing thought,
Prayer, faith and hope—OUR IMMORTALITY!

In these lone paths, eternal twilight round us,
Oh, thou, beginner of existence; thou,
Whose bosom with the restless ardor glows
Of untried expectation; thou, whose life
Hath mournful garb upon it, and whose heart,
Grown weary of its burden, for support
Leans on the staff of Faith—companion, friend,
Youth, manhood, and e'en thou, whose foot-falls reach
The very threshold of Eternity—
Together let us walk, together talk,
And 'neath the solemn arches of these boughs,
That twine, like friendship, in each other's arms,
List to the teachings of the friendly voice
Of the pervading Influence, that doth dwell
Near these dark rocks, by yonder babbling stream,
And in th' uncertain recesses beyond.

How silent, how profound! hush'd—solemn—dim.
Except the whispering of a million leaves
Stirred by the wandering winds, or distant dash
Of rock-born fountains; or, less audible,
The rustling of sere leaves, that, from the boughs
Slowly descending, heap the yellow earth,
All else is still. Like stoic sentinels,
Moss-trunk'd and sinewy-limb'd, gnarl'd, rough and crook'd,
Spreading their century's growth to the blue heaven,
Guarding this solemn place, the old oaks stand.
Yonder the delicate aspen, quivering leaved;
The generous-bearing walnut, and the beech;
The ruby-beaded thorn, and sturdy pine,
Green as affection, and as love enduring.
Weave, with out-spreading boughs a sacred shade.

Stay now; and rest thee in this favorite spot,
Sequestered from the gaze of man; and here,
Beneath the awning of the maple's boughs,

On this cool moss-bank, which o'erlooks the stream,
Sit thee awhile, and drink the influence
Of lovely Nature in her lone retreats.
See, through the net-work of white clouds, the stars,
The pure intelligence of Heaven, look down,
And guide thy thoughts to grandeur: Through the leaves
The night-winds rustle, with a sweet, low sound,
Like spirit-music, such as we have heard
When silver-slippered Fancy tuned her harp
To aerial numbers in the Hall of Dreams,
And Love and Hope, and childhood's blessing, Joy,
Danced to the melody. The ferns and grass
Bend with their load of night dew, and the fount,
That ripples at our feet, tinkles a song
Upon the pebbles, soft as the far chime
Of vesper church-bells trembling in the air.
Be silent; for the Spirit of these groves,
The solemn teacher of our natural faith,
Through visible symbols to thy heart doth speak
Of life, of death and Immortality:—

"A few short years, and thou, and thine, and all
Who claim thy recollection, will go down,
With all the unremembered of the past—
King, prince and peasant; noble, good and vile;
The servant and his master; serf and lord,
Who sleep an equal slumber in the grave—
To be forgotten—to a silent home;
A realm of shades uncertain, and a night,
Eternal in its darkness, where the form,
The palpable essence of your two-fold life,
In still corruption shall resolve to dust,
And give to Nature what it gathered thence.
There, neither joy, nor the tumultuous bliss
Of o'erwrought expectation; nor the fear

Of suffering; **nor the pang** of pain or grief;
Nor disappointment's bitterness are known,
But a pervading peace—a sleep, a rest,
Disturbed by nothing—quietude unbroken.
"To thee, the generations **yet unborn**,
The busy world, and all who do inherit
Or earth, or sea, or air, shall surely move,
Silent as shades that mingle with the night,
And enter with thee the abode of rest.
The records of the past, the lore of mind,
Distinction, grade, the monuments of art,
The wealth, the power, the drama of a world,
Shall be enveloped in that night of sleep.
Ay, all that was of matter, or shall be,
All the material universe, the form,
The substance of all being shall be lost—
Without a trace of likeness passed away,
Like sunbeams on the waste of Ocean's waves,
Lost in infinity of gloom. O night!
Unending, joyless, dreamless night of Peace!

"**Life hath a** two-fold form—that which connects
Material essence with immortal part,
And that of spirit only; but the first,
As doth the natural world, grows to decay.
The bud of being in its germ contains
The elements of its destruction;
And all who breathe, with the first breath they draw,
Inhale a poison which makes death their doom.
Yet fear thou not the sure approach of death;
It is no ' King of Terrors;' fear thou not.
Death hath no shape; it is a formless thing;
The absence of the principle of life;
A blank, a void, which thought can not conceive.
It ends the mystery of life, and solves

The problem of existence. It is *you*
Who clothe it with unsightly forms and shapes,
And in imagination give a birth
To such creations as are bred in fear,
And nourished in the reveries of gloom.

"Behold! the hand of Destiny is here!
You mighty oak, Methuselah in years,
Torn by the fury of the elements,
The victim of a thousand unseen foes,
A fallen monarch, rotteth back to dust,
Its strong heart yielding to a slow decay.
The million leaves that yester-morn were green,
Rejoicing in the sunlight and the breeze,
Beneath thy feet, like hopes in manhood, lie,
Scattered and withered, sere and desolate.
The flowers that blossomed by yon babbling brook,
That blushed in fragrance to the blue of Heaven,
And made delightful all the odorous air,
Faded and hurried to the dust of earth;
But from their stems the germs of life dropped down,
Which, when the spring her vesture shall put on,
And the life-giving Monarch of the skies return,
To heat with ardent breath the senseless mold,
Shall spring to being; bud, unfold and fade,
Yet reproduce their likeness, year by year.

"This Destiny, death's master, fear thou not;
For thou, Oh, man, within thy clayey vestment,
Hast a perennial germ, which, when the robe
Is lain aside—when, with material forms
It sleeps forever—when, with the passing show,
The trappings and appendages which deck
The visible and unsubstantial lost,
In the obscurity of common dust—
SHALL BURST AT ONCE INTO IMMORTAL BLOOM."

BEREAVED.

E walks the earth with downcast eyes,
In which are sorrow and the pain
That softens in heart-easing rain.

The tumult of the busy world,
Its noisy strife and toil, he hears;
It falls upon unheeding ears.

For what to him are greed and gain
Who, mourning like the woodland dove,
Broods o'er the vacant nest of love?

THERE COMES A TIME.

HERE comes a time when we grow old,
　　And like a sunset down the sea
　　Slope gradual, and the night-winds cold
　　Come whispering sad and chillingly;
　　　　And locks are gray
　　　　As winter's day,
And eyes of saddest blue behold
　　The leaves all weary drift away,
　　And lips of faded coral say,
There comes a time when we grow old.

There comes a time when joyous hearts,
　　Which leaped as leaps the laughing main,
Are dead to all save memory,
　　As prisoner in his dungeon chain;
　　　　And dawn of day,
　　　　Hath passed away,
The moon hath into darkness rolled,
　　And, by the embers wan and gray,
　　I hear a voice, in whispers say,
There comes a time when we grow old.

There comes a time when manhood's prime
　　Is shrouded in the mist of years,
And beauty, fading like a dream,
　　Hath passed away in silent tears;
　　　　And then how dark!
　　　　But oh! the spark

That kindled youth to hues of gold,
   Still burns with clear and steady ray,
   And fond affections lingering, say—
There comes a time when we grow old.

There comes a time when laughing Spring
   And golden Summer cease to be,
And we put on the Autumn robe,
   To tread the last declivity;
      But now the slope,
      With rosy Hope,
Beyond the sunset we behold
   Another dawn, with fairer light,
   While watchers whisper through the night—
There comes a time when we grow old.

THE RURAL EDITOR.

OME thou, who taught'st me by the cooling spring,
'Mid pleasant airs and sylvan shades to sing,
Where oft my youthful footsteeps idly strayed.
And numbers rude to ruder songs essayed.
—Alas! in vain I call upon the Muse,
Entreat, invoke—now flatter, now abuse;
Like Baal's stupid gods who wouldn't "peep,"
The ancient virgin must be fast asleep.
In hopeful mood I asked her to inspire
My awkward fingers and unsounded lyre,
And loan a coal from her celestial fire.
She cut me short, and " Poetry," said she,
" Hath its own pure, peculiar pedigree:
It comes, like measles, in a perfect flood,
And, like the measles, runs in certain blood!"

Thus much 'tis proper I should here confess,
Nor claim a talent I do not possess.
You do not look for snows in tropic lands,
Nor flowers nor fruits in wastes of scorching sands.
Much less expect poetic thoughts and views
From one by *you* anointed—not the Muse;
No HARRIS I, who sings whate'er he feels,
With all the Muses flocking at his heels,
Who never asks, and gets uncertain sums,
Nor churns for butter, but the butter comes;
No DODGE, to improvise for you a song—

He finds words ready as he goes along,
And like the Pike's Peak miners—as 'tis told—
From every common clod kicks out the gold.
Yet, since the task is mine for you to rhyme,
This first—I trust the *last* and *only* time—
Like Job, who sang his own afflictions best,
And found experience gave uncommon zest,
Be you indulgent, dull though I may seem,
And be the RURAL EDITOR my theme.

  Unhappy wight! illusion fills his days
Who thinks the occupation ever pays;
And thrice unhappy, who, in quest of fame,
From "rags and lampblack" thinks to earn a name.
He hopes, perhaps, illustrious to shine,
A meteor in the editorial line;
New themes to broach, new projects to advance,
And lead the startled world a dizzy dance;
Perchance to wake, and find himself mistaken.
  When unpropitious hour!—he sighs to see
His last great "leader" wrap the grocer's bacon,
  Or folded round his favorite Bohea.
Fame! if he seeks it, let him volunteer,
  Join Brigham's Saints, or Walker's ragged force,
  Or, what is surer, sue for a divorce,
And run the gauntlet of a gazetteer.
He'd stand a chance at least of notoriety,
In all the circles of our best society,
Find a bad life served up quite newspaporial,
With a worse picture, in the next pictorial.

  Once on a time—so run all tale prefaces—
(I make no mention here of dates or places.)
I knew an Editor—'twas long ago,
Before the art was bless'd by steam or HOE.

When printers dined on unsubstantial fare,
And nursed their hopes on whispers from the air,
Grew rich on poverty, and stuff'd their clay
On airy nothings—promises to pay.
Well, as I said, I knew him—a rare fellow,
Who kept his own and other's natures mellow;
One of those social souls we all enjoy,
Who hold in age the freshness of the boy.
His bright philosophy could brook no fears,
  For he was cheerful as a lad at taw,
And would be, though the world were drowned in tears;
  (O'er a mint julep) happy with a "straw."
He was ambitious, too—I can't say wise,
And though not prudent, full of enterprise;
For 'twas no show of wisdom, you'll confess,
In those sad days to calculate success
From doubtful profits of a country press.
But then he purchased one, with type and cases,
Some ancient racks and stands, and rules and chases,
(They were all second-hand, 'tis well to mention,
And had seen service worthy of a pension.)
And with this outfit, in a rural town,
To life's stern toil he bravely settled down.

Forth came his paper, neatly launched and freighted,
And when it came, the village was elated;
Ignoring party, in a party sense,
Avoiding all that might excite offense.
It praised the town, its prospects, its advances,
Its enterprise, resources and finances;
It praised the schools, the teachers so profound,
Until their fame was known for miles around;
It praised the village parson's eloquence,
His modest bearing, lack of all pretense;
But most his learning and his solid sense;

So it fell out, between the spring and fall,
That worthy from the city had a call,
With such an offer for his preachéd word,
That he felt sure that call was from the Lord;
It praised the doctors as uncommon skill'd,
  Adding with great suaviter and grace,
Their treatment cured more people than it kill'd;
It spoke—and of its truth some doubts will spring—
Of honest lawyers—an uncommon thing—
  Who had a conscience—an uncommon case.
In short, it praised so well, that people grew
To think *that praise* was merited and due;
It was his fault, and grew from an excess
Of aim to please and profit—nothing less;
And had he been to self but half the friend
He was to others, he had met an end
That *you* might safely aim at and commend.

  His influence was felt—the town's fair fame,
With all who read his paper, found a name;
The city pleasurists resorted there,
Enjoyed its quiet and its healthy air;
The artists came, and sketched such charming scenes
That they were sought to grace the magazines;
And thither too, came men of enterprise—
Blocks rose on blocks, and mills and factories,
Hotels palatial, and stores that vied
With those on Broadway, or along Cheapside.
In brief the town, that ere the printer came,
Had scarce "a local habitation or a name,"
As though 'twere touched by magic, grew to be
An inland city—but how flourished he?

Come with me, up three flights of stairs, and there,
In dingy daylight and lead-poisoned air,
Beside his desk he sits, his hair has grown
Gray with the flecks that time and care have sown;

Around him lie exchanges, scraps and clippings,
Half written leaders, locals, puffs and sippings
Of *Punch*-y humor; manuscripts rejected,
From geniuses who think themselves neglected;
Obituary verses, full of gloom,
And doleful voices from a doleful tomb;
"Lines to a Lady," from a Mister Dash,
Who's desp'rately in love with—his moustache;
A sentimental song about sea-shells,
  Writ by a moping, melancholy she,
Who would be married, though her face yet smells
  Of bread-and-butter and the nursery;

An eulogy on General Blank's oration,
Delivered off-hand at the late ovation,
And which suggests, by way of mere reflection,
He should be honored with a re-election;
Modest requests, which hope he'll not refuse
To notice this or that in next week's *News;*
A bunch of bad segars, that some one sends,
  Expecting thrice their value in a local;
Unopened invitations from his friends,
  Asking his presence at a concert vocal,
Or at a lecture, party, hop or ball,
At such a date (please mention) and such hall;
Novels and books not worth a decent rating,
  Sent out—they send few others but for cash—
By eastern firms, who take that way of baiting,
  The country press to advertise their trash;
In short, an hundred things by men devised
To get their baubles cheaply advertised.

There, patient toiler! ever at his work,
Himself his foreman, publisher and clerk,
He labored hard—few men had labored harder—
Grew lean in person, leaner in his larder;
And still he toiled, from dawn to twilight gray,
The first of men to court—*the last to pay!*
Some said that he was rich—it might be true,
Provided that you reckoned what was due;
But this his dearest friends both said and knew—
His wants were many, but his dimes were few.
His paper-bills came in, which *must* be paid,
So, to delinquents he appealed for aid;
He would take pork, potatoes, corn or oats,
Axe-helves or hoop-poles, or, at worst, their notes;
In short, take anything they had to pay,
Provided it was brought by such a day.

And thus he turned short corners, always pressed,
   A sad example of POPE's sagest saw,
"Man never is, but always to be blessed,"
   The victim of a fate that knows no law.
Beset by butchers, by his baker teased,
By creditors besieged, by bailiffs squeezed,
He yielded slowly, in the desperate strife,
His dingy office and his troubled life,
And gave to quiet earth and modest stones
His many virtues and his aching bones.
Some generous friends have built a cenotaph
   Of spotless marble o'er the sleeper's dust,
On which the passer reads this epitaph:

"HERE LIES A MAN WHO DIED OF TOO MUCH TRUST!"

   'Tis a plain story, rather roughly told,
Of one who trusted others and was "sold;"
By hope allured, in turn by fear assailed,
He gave to credit all he had, and failed.
The moral *you* can draw. The Country Press
Should seek for independence—nothing less.
Ready to aid the good, sustain the wise,
Direct and counsel proper enterprise,
Revealing to the public gaze the way
Where toil may profit, and where skill will pay.
Where revenues are reaped and fortunes grown,
It should be careful to preserve its own.

   The Country Press! though limited its sphere
Of influence, demands attention here.
Where it is free, the people will be free;
   Where it is pure, the people will be pure;
Where shines its light, there liberty shall be;
   Where it stands firm, there freedom shall endure.

In the great march of mind it leads the van,
The guard of public right, the friend of man.
Though humble toilers, they are not the least
Who sow the seed and garner for the feast;
By little means the noblest ends are gained,
By small advances victories attained.
Look to the sea; from out its wastes arise
Fair isles of beauty, kissed by summer skies.
Mere specks at first, they part the rippling seas;
Bald, barren rocks then rise by slow degrees,
And here extends a shoal, and there an arm,
Here swells a hill, there sinks a valley warm:
Along its beach clings fast the floating weed,
And spicy winds waft down the feathery seed;
To ardent suns succeed the gentle rains,
Green grow the hills and flowers adorn the plains:
Fair trees spring up to whisper with the breeze,
And flashing fountains leap to join the seas,
Where birds of song with sweetest music come,
And build their nests and make their happy home.
And there it stands! a glory mid the isles,
Where spring eternal sheds her sweetest smiles;
Through centuries its builders toiled to raise
Another Eden in the later days;
A new creation under heaven's dome,
Where Love might dwell and Virtue find a home.
Their toil was humble 'neath a surging flood,
Their aim was noble and the end was good.

O, humble toilers! ye who guide the press,
Though slow the progress, sure will be success.
Patient in labor, strong in hope; in faith
Outreaching time and circumstance and death;
Be yours the aim, by heaven at first designed,
To raise to higher range of thought the mind;

Building amid the floods of selfish life,
The storms of passion and the waves of strife,
A fairer island in each human soul,
Where Love shall dwell and Virtue have control.
An Eden blessed, and fairer than the old,
By poets sung, by prophet lips foretold,
The home of Innocence, Religion's shrine,
Where God may reign and Man become divine.

IN MEMORY.

THE robin rests its northward wing,
    And twittering in the quickened tree,
    Pipes all its sweetest notes for me—
The merriest prophet of the spring.

I knew that it would come once more
    When nights grew short and days were long
    To wake the morning with its song,
And feed its fledgelings round my door.

From all the fields the snows have fled,
    And thro' the grasses gray and sere,
    Peeps the green promise of the year—
The hope that slumbered with the dead.

In every nook the crocus springs—
    The dandelions star the hills,
    And round the golden daffodils
I hear the bee's industrious wings.

O soon the frolic June will come
    And shake her flaunting roses out,
    And woods be gay with song and shout
And not a voice on earth be dumb.

Alas! for those who mourn and stand
    Like watchers by a rainy sea,
    Who wait for what may never be,
The white sails striving for the land.

Their prayers are sighs, their vows are tears,
    For sorrow stayeth all the night,
    And sorrow broodeth in the light,
And casts her shadow through the years.

        *   *

The ash leaf reddens to its fall,
    The nights are long, the days are drear,
    And hastening to its end, the year
With frosty fingers weaves its pall.

When like a youth in bloom it came,
    And flaunted all its garlands out,
    And woods were filled with song and shout
And thorns wore coronals of flame —

When gladness poured like crusted wine
    From June's delicious beaker, then
    He walked among the sons of men,
Dear to all hearts, but most to thine.

A NEW YEAR'S RHYME.

1864.

I.

WE live and love and laugh and weep and die;
    The years add nothing to the simple story.
And what comes after? Neither you nor I,
    Who stand upon time's jutting promontory
And seaward gaze, to watch life's ships go by,
    Freighted with love, hope, hate, joy, grief and glory,
Can say what shores they visit, or what gales
Blow prosperous, or tear their shining sails.

II.

For none return of all that pass the dim
    Horizon, sinking from our saddened sight;
We hear the rippling keel, the sailor's hymn,
    Exchange the passing hail, the fond good night,
And watch till in the distance seems to swim
    The signal lamp of love and life and light—
A very star its twinkling radiance glows,
Then vanishes—but where? No mortal knows.

III.

If thus the bard begins, the occasion pricks his
    Conscience to 't. Death takes a thousand guises:
Deceitful fevers, troublesome asphyxies,
    Tormenting pangs and horrible surprises,

And shapes more hideous still in savage Dixie's
  Blood-sodden fields, where many a soldier lies, his
Head blown off to satisfy war's licenses
In one of our most famous reconnoissances.

IV.

Dear are remembered pleasures :—dear the kiss
  That modest love first snatched from lips untainted;
Dear boyhood's homes and haunts; the friends we miss,
  Whose names the marble bears, whose souls are sainted;
But dearer far than these, than all, I wis,
  That rosy fancy e'er illuminated,
Are thoughts of tender hands and loving eyes
To the brave soldier in his agonies.

V.

What then to him the drum-beat, and the blare
  Of bugles, or th' impetuous shock of war
When raging armies mingle, and red glare
  The volleying lines, and, like a pestilent star,
The howling shell bursts through the smoking air,
  And scatters death around him and afar?
To him alike are friend and foe, who hears
The battle-clamor ring in dying ears.

VI.

No more the light tattoo shall bid him rest,
  And distant bugles lull to slumbers deep;
The musket to his side is feebly press'd
  By hands still faithful to the charge they keep;
And oozing from the calm, heroic breast,
  Life slips away into eternal sleep.
But O, the death-pang that shall break the hearts
Of those who love, when such a soul departs!

VII.

Come, Peace, with healing on thy sacred wings,
  Love in thy breast, and promise in thine eyes;
To thee the mourning heart exultant springs,
  To thee the fainting soul rejoicing flies.
Come! By the blasted hearth no longer sings
  The merry cricket. Bid the cottage rise;
Rebuild the hearth; the wasted lands restore,
And curl the vines 'round every happy door.

VIII.

Under thy gentle reign we'll beat our spears
  To pruning-hooks, our swords to prospering plows;
Keep for parades our surplus Brigadiers,
  And thatch their bomb-proof heads with laurel boughs;
Have all contractors shot by volunteers;
  Hang those who steal more than the law allows;
Give Merit office, order Truth a bust,
And swear to honest incomes—if we must!

IX.

Deliver us from draft, debt and the devil,
  The tax collector, and the provost guard;
On money-changers, who refuse to level
  Greenbacks and gold, be thou exceeding hard;
In thy great mercy take them from this evil,
  Misbegotten world, and great be thy reward!
Not, Maid of Olives, that we lust for lucre,
Or cheat at any game ourselves but euchre.

X.

For we're indifferent honest—say the least—
  Stick to our sects, our parties and gregarious
Professions, whereby men are skinned and fleeced,
  Through arts as wondrous as they're neat and various;

We pay our doctor roundly and our priest,
    The one to kill, the other prompt to bury us;
And when we can not lodge him unawares,
We kick the devil down the kitchen stairs.

XI.

We are not as the heathen herd who bend
    The knee to Baal, and live in huts and caves,
Who, when they have a killing of foe and friend,
    Feed on their flesh to save the expense of graves.
We pity them afar-off, and we send
    Bibles and missionaries to the knaves,
To teach them that among us 'tis as common a
Thing,—but not so bad if done by Jomini.

XII.

We keep the ten commandments, and we keep
    The 'leventh also, when our neighbors let us;
We doubly love them if their purse be deep,
    And in their testaments they don't forget us;
But we can't love the negro, though he steep
    His skin in all the sweet dews of Hymettus,
Or own a clam-bank stretch'd—well, for that matter as
Far's Pass'maquoddy's distant from Cape Hatteras.

XIII.

If, therefore, we're afflicted for his sake,
    Hence from our sight, fair Maid of Olives, fly!
What can a martyr suffer more than bake,
    Or what a white man more than fight and die?
Our chance in war another year will take,
    And Richmond also—leastwise, we will try.
And if with Grant to lead we can't go through it,
Then never will a Yankee-doodle do it.*

XIV.

The war must end . . . and so must end this verse.
   If you're the better for it, it is well;
If not, thank Heaven there's nothing in it worse.
   Farewell the sandal-shoon, the scallop shell!
Vain world adieu!—a blessing or a curse
   Would make no difference;—and so farewell
Peace, War, Love, Hatred, Joy and Tears:
Ye are the wretched substance of the Years.

---

* See Fitz Green Halleck's "Fanny."

THE FARMER.

HE dwells among the rugged hills,
    And tills the fertile soil;
His hands are hard, his muscles knit
    To manliness, by toil.
He may not have the easy grace
    That fashion can impart,
But in his sun-browned face is seen
    The goodness of his heart;
And few of those who walk the sod
Are better noblemen of God.

Trained up in blamelessness of thought,
    He leads a happy life;
His heart is in his peaceful home,
    His ways averse to strife.
Free as the air that cools his brow,
    He spurns oppression's rod;
His rule of life—true love to man,
    Implicit faith in God.
Hope ever proves his faithful friend,
And all his acts his life commend.

Years will depart, and cares increase,
    His form be bowed with age—
Yet nought diminish of the man,
    While adding to the sage.
And they shall say of him, when dead—
    And say without constraint:
"So bright an ornament to man
    Is canonized a Saint:
And few who on our earth have trod
Were better noblemen of God."

BY THE SEA-SIDE.

THE sound of the surf of the sand-making ocean,
   The sails of the ships on the shimmering sea,
Bring back to my mind the long days of devotion
   I gave by the sea-side to love and to thee.

'Twas homage man pays, and but once, to a woman,
   A love that would forfeit the world for a kiss,
Ay, and heaven itself, with its joys superhuman,
   To catch from her smile but one moment of bliss.

How strong was the spell of thy presence! Days ended
   In weeks, and weeks glided to months of repose;
And time—it was measured by sunbeams that blended
   Their light with the dew and the pink of the rose.

Well, 'tis past! that wild waltz of the heart, to whose measure
   Love's pulses beat madly, till being became
A thing of too exquisite rapture for pleasure,
   And sharper than hunger, and fiercer than flame.

I chide thee! No, no! Let them bear all the shame of it
  Who chilled thy young heart with an infinite fear;
I forget not, though rashly I gave thee the blame of it,
  That the spoil of a heart was atoned by a tear.

Like a bride of the East in her splendor they made thee,
  With cluster of jewels and cunning of gold;
Had they seen in what robes the dark years have arrayed thee,
  Nor wealth would have purchased, nor beauty been sold.

Men worshipped, maids envied, as up to the altar,
  Pale wonder of sweetness, they led thee a bride,
Nor dreamed they who heard thy lips quiver and falter,
  That the flower of thy young life there withered and died.

And now, like the perfume of roses long faded,
  That vision of loveliness comes from the past,
But the eyes that entreated, the lips that upbraided,
  No more shall reproach thee—O, broken at last!

Should the sails of these ships by the tempest be shredded,
  The strong ribs be crushed by the sea in its rage,
The wreck were no greater than thine, who wert wedded,
  To folly in youth and misfortune in age.

What haunt of the city conceals thy grey sorrow?
  Thy children they cry in the streets for their bread;
And for thee there remains no bright hope for the morrow,
  But only the peace of the sleep of the dead.

SONNET.

HILD of my heart! Ideal of my dreams!
   Thou pattern of all gentleness and love!
   My heart flies to thee, as the pining dove
   Flies to its mate; and when life busiest seems,
   And the hot brain, o'ertasked with thickening schemes,
Reels with perplexities, one thought of thee,
One blesséd thought, that thou dost keep for me
Thy heart's choice treasures, e'en as limpid streams
Their cooling waters for the parching plains;
   That in thy heart's most consecrated shrine
   I have a dwelling place, most fondly mine,
Straightway my soul her wonted power regains,
And Hope's bright promises upon me shine
In the sweet consciousness that thou art wholly mine.

THE FOUNTAIN IN THE WILDERNESS.

O Fons Blandusiæ! splendidior vitro.—HORAT.

IN this uncultivated wild,
   Where Nature's lavish hand is seen,
The gloomy, tender, rugged, mild,
   Profusion's endless change of green,
     One charm alone could add a grace,
       Adorn, refresh, sustain and bless,
     And that—the beauty of the place—
       The fountain in the wilderness.

From the cleft granite in the hill,
   Whose jutting front gnarled roots entwine.
Through fissures numberless distill
   Thy waters, Fountain of the Pine!
What skill hath wrought thy urn of white,
   And crowned its rim with flowers, whose hue
     Is varied as the rainbow's light,
       And as the rainbow, transient, too.

Calm, placid fountain! who can gaze
   In thy clear waters, and behold
The mid-day sun's untarnished rays
   Reflected back in hues of gold,
And not rejoice that heavenly worth,
   Though found in plain and humble guise,
May send its brilliancy from earth
   In heightened splendor to the skies.

How pure, how lucent, how serene,
    Thy ceaseless waters leap to light,
Like crystal in the sunlight seen,
    Whose brightness dazzles on the sight.
Thou prototype of purity!
    Of peace th' example 'mid unrest,
O, teach me what the heart may be
    By virtue, love and peace possess'd.

In ages past, ere yet the East
    Had heard of our far western world;
Ere kingdoms rose, that since have ceased,
    And empires — since in ruin hurled;
Calmly thy waters welled to view,
    And glided through their pebbled way,
Reflecting heaven's unfading blue
    As clear and truly as to-day.

The antlered deer and timid doe
    Came hither in the olden days,
And on thy even face below
    Delighted much and long to gaze;
And of thy limpid waters quaff'd,
    While fawns in transports bounded by,
Safe from the quick, invidious shaft,
    And the red huntsman's searching eye.

Here, too, the tawny lovers came,
    And wooed in accents now unknown,
When the round moon — a shield of flame —
    In summer's milder evenings shone.
What raptures, what delights of love,
    Melted and thrilled the savage breast,
When lips, that torture could not move,
    Faltered with vows half unexpressed.

The music of thy flow, how sweet
    To their untuned, untutored ears,
While they, in turn, the tale repeat
    Of cherished hopes and vanished fears.
Thy ripple low, the winds above,
    The swaying boughs, the sighing streams,
Repeat the story of their love,
    Till love in every murmur seems.

I see him now! the warrior chief,
    Proud, haughty, stern, the fearless foe,
Whose vengeance is a kept belief,
    Whose rage, no momentary glow—
Retreating from the hard-fought field,
    Defiance flashing from his eye,
Though vanquished, yet untaught to yield,
    Though conquered, yet disdains to fly:

I see him, thirsty, bleeding, haste
    To thee, O Fountain of the Pine!
(How sweet thy cooling balm to taste,
    And on thy flowery verge recline:)
He kneels! he drinks! O blessed fount!
    How quick to cool heat's raging flame,
T' allay, to soothe, if not surmount,
    The pangs that rack his quivering frame.

No more revenge, like poison, burns,
    Nor rage, nor hatred fires his breast;
To heaven his eye undaunted turns,
    And to his brow his hand is press'd.
His heart is with his thoughts, and they —
    Unchanged in death as fixed through life —
Are with his children now at play,
    And her, his dark-eyed Indian wife.

THE FOUNTAIN IN THE WILDERNESS.

These scenes have passed: no more beside
  Thy pleasant waters shall they meet,
The tawny lover and his bride,
  To woo and wed in accents sweet;
No more the huntsman's shaft shall pierce
  The antlered deer and timid doe,
Nor hostile chiefs, in conflict fierce,
  Shout triumph o'er a prostrate foe.

Perished a race that well deserved
  A better fate, a lasting name;
No record of those deeds preserved,
  That well were worth eternal fame:
To them no tribute do we pay—
  Those heroes of the olden days!
Except such sympathy as may
  Adorn a poet's idle lays.

But thou, O fountain!—tranquil fount!
  Hast seen them: would thou hadst a tongue,
Their perished hist'ry to recount,
  What tales they told, what heroes sung.

Canst thou the secret not disclose?
  Vain babbler! what to thee were they?
Or what am I who now propose
  Such questions? canst thou tell me? say.

O Fountain in the Wilderness!
  Henceforth let others learn from thee:
Not all we see should we confess,
  Nor all confess that others see.
To harbor peace within the breast,
  To draw from all their sweetest grace;
Like thee, be calm amid unrest,
  And wear, like thee, a pleasant face.

THE UNRETURNING.

SPRING comes again in beauty unto earth,
In all her recesses of light and shade,
The joy of sunshine and the mellow rain.
E'en querulous Age, leaning upon his staff,
Peers from dim eyes to welcome her return,
And wrinkles his lean features into smiles;
And lusty youth, with song and madrigal,
Goes forth to meet her in the budding groves,
And with rejoicings, follows where her steps
Awake the slumbering beauty of the flowers.
No more, O! never more, will her return
Bring back the joys of recollected days,
Though, sitting on the sun-crowned hill, she sing
"Rejoice, rejoice, O Love, rejoice with me!
Rejoice and come with me, for now the fir
Drops balsam, and the tender leaf appears,
The sweet young corn puts out its tiny blade,
The elm its buds, and every vine its green;
Rejoice and come with me; the coppice yields
The balm of waxen calyx swol'n with life,
And all the dells are fiery with the rose,
And all the meres with cowslips turn to gold.
"Rejoice, rejoice, O Love, rejoice with me!"
No more th' accustomed haunt, the populous grove,
Full of young life and old decay, where glint
Innumerable wings through interlacing boughs,
Shall he revisit for whom love now mourns,
Sitting with folded wings beside his grave;
Who waned in dawning, like a morning star,
In the full flush of the unclouded day.

AS I LOVE.

O you love as I love?
   Do you cherish the flame
   That trembles to brightness
    At thought of her name?
  Is it secret, confiding,
Unshaken, abiding,
All frailties hiding?
  Then you love as I love.

Do you love as I love?
  Do your thoughts ever run,
Like rivers to ocean,
  To center in one?
Is it constant, concealing
In words, not in feeling,
But in blushes revealing?
  Then you love as I love.

MORNING ON MARYLAND HIGHTS.

[1862.]

STAR of the rosy dawn, upon thy face
The shepherds of Chaldea turned their eyes,
As o'er the windy hills their flocks they led,
And glimmering up the misty steeps of night
The faint dawn trembled, till the luminous air
Took to itself thy glory, and afar
On crest and cliff and solemn pinnacle
Burned the full splendor of the risen morn.
Their eyes behold thee not, but still thy path
Thou hold'st in heaven, and still thy holy beams
Shine on the faces and the homes of men.
They came and worshipped thee, and passed away—
Before them thou, and thou when they were not.

The fire-eyed eagle, clasping with lean claws
The wint'ry crag that earliest takes the sun,
Ere yet the rounded world swings full to thee,
Or the white morning's glistening sandals track
The mountain slopes, lifts his imperial wing,
And, through the infinite blue, a lessening form
Goes forth to meet thee on thy rosy way.
The old woods and the ancient solitudes
Thy influence feel; and when with gracious light
Thou fillest the hazy spaces of the East,
The brooding spirit of the Almighty moves
The billowy depths of ocean and of air,
And the majestic wilderness rolls back
The sounding anthem of the chanting sea.

How like a spirit of light thou springest up,
Leading the archer with his silver bow
And quiver of night-scattering arrows, o'er
These rugged hights, whose everlasting fronts
Stand sentinel to the pathways of the world.
Or whether named of him, (as poets feign)
The charmed astronomer who nightly viewed
The circling heavens from Atlas; nor had ceased
Till now his patient vigils on that lonely mount,
But by an horrid tempest seized, was whirled
Through howling darkness to the void:—or called
Of that fair boy the sea-born beauty wooed
With kisses and entreaties in the groves
Of famed Idalia:—thou art still the same
Unto the redbreast that, from thickets wild,
Singest thy coming. Neither he alone:
The wilderness awakes, and from its depths
The angels of the morning call to thee.
The children of the mountain and the vale,
The old divinities of groves and streams,
Th' inhabitants of animate wilds, fair forms
Of grace and beauty, born of heaven to dwell
By cooling fountains and in forest glades,
Rejoice in thee, and through the pleasant land
Make merry morning, breathing unto thee
The feasting sweetness of Arcadian flutes.

II.

Fair is thy light, and fair the tender dawn
Thou usherest in—alas! no more to bring
The days when Peace went singing through the land.
No more, O frosty Loudon, from thy hights
Descending to the sea-green river's shore,
Nor yet by thee, watering a fruitful vale,
Bright Shenandoah, shall she come to dwell,

Pleas'd with the fattening herds, the prospering share,
And the young corn with promise bourgeoning out.
War's trumpets wake the hills, and volleying roll
The throbbing thunders of contending guns;
The far-off mountains, purple-peaked or veiled
In deeper blue than heaven, send harshly back
Their angry echoes, roaring through the vale.

O mother of the mighty dead! who hast
In thy blind rage reversed thy glorious shield,
Exalting over Liberty the heel
Of the mail'd Despot, how shalt thou repent
In tears and blood thy unexampled crime.
No happy star leads up thy day of peace.
But, miserable, from thy stormy skies
Rain famine, pestilence and death, as once
The Florentine beheld, in nether woe,
Dilated flakes of slow-consuming marl
Fall scorching on th' unhappy, doom'd to fire.
As thou that sittest in the clefted rocks,
Once haughty village, shall her cities be,
And o'er deserted streets and shattered walls
Shall Desolation reign with stony eye,
To smite her children with remorse and shame,
Remembering how, to foul rebellion given,
Ungodly lust of power, and pride of blood,
They lost the priceless heritage of man—
The unity of liberty and law.

But thou, fair star, that even as I gaze,
Dost fade in light more glorious than thine own,
Be thou the emblem of my Fatherland.
Though round these hights the bellowing tempest break,
And from its rocky bed the whirlwind tear
The sinewy oak and twist the pliant fir,

And like the gloomy smoke of battle whirl,
From steaming gorges and surcharged ravines,
The pluming mists, through which the lightnings leap
A tangled flame—thou, in thy sphere serene,
Rollest in light, obscured but never dimmed,
Above the warring elements, and bring'st
Day, and the golden calm of summer skies,
To be a sweet awakening to the world.

SUMMER DAYS.

N summer, when the day's were long,
    We walked together in the wood;
Our heart was light, our step was strong;
    Sweet flutterings then were in our blood,
In summer when the days were long.

We strayed from morn till evening came;
    We gathered flowers and wove us crowns;
We walked 'mid poppies red as flame,
    Or sat upon the yellow downs;
And always wished our lives the same.

In summer, when the days were long,
    We leaped the hedge-row, crossed the brook;
And still her voice flowed forth in song,
    Or else she read some graceful book,
In summer when the days were long.

And then we sat beneath the trees,
    With shadows lessening in the noon;
And in the sunlight and the breeze
    We rested many a gorgeous June,
While larks were singing o'er the leas.

We loved, and yet we knew it not—
    For loving seemed like breathing then;
We found a heaven in every spot;
    Saw angels, too, in all good men,
And dreamed of God in grove and grot.

SUMMER DAYS.

In summer, when the days were long,
    Alone I wander,—muse alone—
I see her not; but that old song
    Under the fragrant wind is blown,
In summer when the days are long.

Alone I wander in the wood;
    But one fair spirit hears my sighs;
And half I see, so glad and good,
    The honest daylight of her eyes,
That charmed me under earlier skies.

In summer, when the days are long,
    I love her as we loved of old;
My heart is light, my step is strong;
    For love brings back those hours of gold
In summer when the days are long.

A SUBURBAN HOME.

Happy is he who hath his chosen home
Set in a corner of the noisy world
Not so remote from business and the marts
Wherein all commerce thrives, as to have lost
Man's interest in men, nor yet so near
As quite to lose remembrance of clear skies,
The infinite tenderness of heaven's blue,
And the fresh world that year by year renews
An Eden lovely as the angels saw
Who guarded its white gates with flaming swords.

THE AVOWAL.

IF love be the devotion of a soul,
  That, with the world to choose from, yet returns
  Slave of thy wish, and prisoner at thy will,
And bids thee bind him with thy stronger chain,
Then love I thee; and lacking fitter words,
Mine actions leave to plead my further cause.

PROTEAN DUST.

OR whether on the mountain height,
   Or in the valley deep,
  It matters not, where falls the night,
   When weary mortals sleep
Their final sleep. Their dust shall be
  The dust of other men,
And mixed in Nature's alchemy,
  Yet walk the earth again.
In vain the loftiest pyramid,
  The costliest crypt and tomb;
The earth that vanity has hid,
  Shall add to leaf and bloom.
The monarch's dust, perchance, shall feed
  The peasant's violet,
The beggar's from its suffering freed,
  In royal halls be set.

THE EARLY DEAD.

They grow not old, the loved who perish young:
They are forever beautiful: the years,
The blight of sorrow, and the waste of grief,
The canker of affliction and the cares
That creep on our decrepitude, may wreak
On us their ravages, until, o'erspent,
The weary frame drops stiffened to the dust;
But they who, in the blossom of their years,
Depart in all their glory, and go down
In the full flush of beauty to the grave,
Can never know the slow decline of age;
It hath no power upon them; but, afar,
Transplanted to the Paradise of Faith,
And made immortal in their innocence,
Their purity and loveliness, they bloom,
Rare as the fruits of famed Hesperides,
Beyond the changes and the wrath of Time.

They grow not old, the loved who perish young;
Though in the valleys green where lie their forms
At sleep among the daisies, the heapèd mounds
Sink level with the surface of the plain,
And the white stone, the kind memorial
Of mourning love for a departed love,
Gathers upon its face the mold of years;
E'en though their resting-place the trackless winds
May seek, but vainly; and the plow-boy turn
With the bright share the turf above their rest.

Unconscious, as he sings his roundelay,
Of forms than his more fair that sleep below
Still, in our hearts they hold remembrance,
And in our dreams do they revisit us;
And through the golden glory of the Past,
Like pictures mellowed by the glaze of age,
The patterns of the beauty still appear
More precious as they seem to gather grace,
More beautiful as we decay; as we grow old,
More dearly loved for memories they bring.

I now bethink me of a gentle one,
So pure she might be canonized a saint,
Who came to us as an exceeding joy,
Who left us in a most exceeding grief.
She was our lily; and the angels loved it,
Who did divide with us a tender charge
Until it budded; and we hoped to see
The beauty of its blossom. But, one day
In the deep glory of a flowering May,
The bright immortals from the Hills of Bliss
Came down into the garden of our love;
And so did they prefer that perfect bud,
And so enamored were they of its grace,
And so they valued it above all others,
That they did breathe upon it; and our lily
Became, henceforth, immortal in its bloom.

A RETROSPECT.

ACKWARD o'er the past I look,
And, as written in a book,
All my life before me lies.
Seal, O Heaven, its mysteries!
Let no eye its pages scan
Without charity for man;
Let no tongue its secrets tell
That love hath not tempered well.
Let no judge, with mien severe,
On my acts hold inquest here.
Lord of Life! thou knowest best—
In thy mercy will I rest.

HOME.

O him who is aweary of the strife,
The disappointment after arduous toil—
Which is ambition's fruit; who wears the weeds
Of rooted sorrows for his vanished hopes;
Whose young desires have changed to stern resolves;
Who looks on life, as the experienced brave
Upon the battle-field—to such, how sweet,
How more than holy is the tender light,
Lingering like flame on a deserted shrine,
Around the spot where Peace nursed his young soul
In the untroubled lap of Innocence!
O, if the heart *can* cling, amid the change,
The wreck and desolation of all things,
With the true fondness of a mother's love,
To anything—of time, of form or place—
To anything worth human adoration,
It is to HOME—the circle of all joys,
The charm of Heaven, the talisman of hearts!
Sweet to the seaman's eye when from afar,
After long voyages on tempestuous seas,
Through indistinctness visible, the hills,
Dear to his heart by many memories—
The blue-crowned hills, amid whose peaceful vales
Nestles in sunshine his parental roof,
First o'er the waters rise upon his sight.
Sweet to the pilgrim, long in stranger lands,
Though it be humble as a wrecker's cot,
The welcome outlines of his early home.

The reverend patriarch—who went forth from thence
Strong in the manhood of untarnished hopes—
Beholds with fondness and a child's delight,
The homely walls that guarded from the world
His helplessness and his unfolding prime.
Dear to the matron—who went forth from thence
Crowned with the garlands of a virgin bride,
Amid the mirth of rustic revelry,
The greetings of young hearts and happy lips—
Is her return to the sequestered spot,
When, like the roses by the moss-grown wall,
She blushed to beauty 'midst its rural charms.
Once more in childhood's home! O, blest retreat!
Asylum for the weary-worn of life,
Thou refuge for the broken-hearted child,
Restorer of lost peace to troubled breasts,
Thou kind protector of insulted worth,
Friend of the hapless whom the world reviles,
The temple and the guardian of love;
Thou Paradise on earth, whose portals close
Against the bitterness of strife and scorn,
Against the rudeness of a selfish world,

Against unfeeling jeers and cold repulse,
Against all that makes misery more deep,
Or mars the happiness of virtuous joy—
What charms like thine can bind the heart of man,
With spells of pleasant memories and dreams,
To hallow with the reverence of love,
Above all other objects of desire,
The altar of the household of his youth?

ELLULA.

ROSY, cheerful, happy child
Was Ellula of the wild!
Raised where naught but forests are
By a hardy forester,
All unknown to other eyes
Than the stars that gem the skies;
Nightingale of Northern bowers,
Queen and sister to the flowers;
Nimble, timid as a fawn,
Lightly leaping o'er a lawn;
Cheeks as ruddy as the dawn;
Parian brow, where curls of gold
Wavy, wanton, richly rolled;
Eyes as blue as skies above,
Liquid, lucent, lurking love;
Heart of charity, and tongue
Never speaking others' wrong;
Voice whose every note was song—
Such was my Ellula, when
Sober Autumn came again,—
Like a hermit penance keeping,
O'er his sins forever weeping—
Then with birds my darling flew
To a fairer climate too.

How much beauty, how much worth
Death hath taken from our earth!
What a gift to us was given!
What a gift returned to Heaven!

Like a star in light expiring,
At the sun's approach retiring,
Leaving us her name to bless,
Leaving earth an angel less,
Giving Heaven an angel more—
Better never passed before,
Either martyr, saint or maiden
With the balm for sorrow laden,
Through the blissful gates of Aidenn.

Sweet Ellula, blest Ellula,
To the spring-perennial Beulah,
To the realm of love and song,
Where was never thought a wrong,
Thou art gone.—Yet, though so dear,
I would never wish thee here,
Never—though the wish were love—
Wish thee from thy bliss above.
I shall greet thee—not with fear :
I shall meet thee—but not here—
Greet thee—where no cares can thwart us :
Meet thee—where no foes can part us.
I shall come with joy to thee :
Thou, in sorrow, ne'er to me.
Till that hour, my life will be
All a dream of Heaven and thee.

THE FLOWER ANGELS.

PON the seven-hued iris sits the queen
Of dews, the diamonds that the tearful naiads bear,
In elfin urns, to jewel all the flowers:
The crimped petals of the tinted buds
They, leaf by leaf unfold, and bend the rays
Of the rich sunlight on their tiny heads,
And with their delicate wings fan the fresh air
On the unconscious beauties, as a mother bends
And breathes upon the features of her sleeping child.

WAITING TO DIE.

ONELY the hearthstone,
    Silent the halls,
Faded the pictures
    Hung on the walls.
Rusty the door-hinge,
    Pathways grass-grown—
O, it is weary
    Dwelling alone!

Sadly he goeth—
Thus do they say—
Locks, once an auburn,
Silvered and gray;
Feebly he's leaning
Now on his cane,
Wrinkled with sorrows,
Bending with pain.

Heavily stepping,
Stiffened with years,
Sightless his dark eyes,
Deafened his ears.
Slowly he moveth—
Let him pass by!
Pity an old man
Waiting to die.

THE LOVED ONES AFAR.

[SONG.]

I.

HEN night winds are wailing,
    Like spirits in thrall,
And death walks in darkness
    Through hamlet and hall;
Kind Angels of Mercy,
    Wherever they are,
Watch over the slumbers
    Of loved ones afar—
Our heart's dearest treasures,
    The loved ones afar.

II.

Where'er they may wander,
    O'er land or o'er sea,
Thou, Father of Angels,
    We trust them with thee!
Be Thou to earth's pilgrims
    The day-beam and star,
The staff of the weary
    To loved ones afar.

III.

While life hath a pleasure,
    Or hope hath a cheer;
While the heart can feel kindness,
    Or sorrow a tear;

I can not forget them,
    Nor fail in the prayer,
That God will watch over
    The loved ones afar.

IV.

The winter of life-time
    May close round in gloom,
And spring flowers may scatter
    Their leaves o'er my tomb;
Yet still, through the darkness,
    Like evening's pale star,
My spirit will hover
    O'er loved ones afar—
Our heart's dearest treasures,
    The loved ones afar.

OCTOBER.

GAZING o'er the wasted lands,
Fallow fields and frosted sands,
Brown October sadly stands
Ankle-deep in leaves that strew
Wood-land walks and valleys low.

THE UNSEALED FUTURE.

TURN not from us, Immortal, thy calm face,
Nor in dull ears receive our fervent prayer.
With clear, cold eyes the years to come thou seest,
The secrets that they hold, and all our fates.
Unseal thy lips, fixed as the Phidian Jove's,
Or with thy bloodless finger to our eyes
Trace the eternal will, the stern decree,
That makes or mars our lives that are to be.
Say to what end we live, that knowing this
We may conform the order of our lives,
Nor blindly work the folly of our wills.

SONG OF PARTING.

WHILE the sad hour is flying,
  How dear the spot appears,
Where love, with flowers undying,
  Crowned all our happy years.
Companion dear, forgive the tear
  That falls o'er pleasures wasting:
Earth has no cheer when thou'rt not near,
  Nor life a bliss worth tasting.

Could fond desire detain thee
  Or Love the moments stay,
Affection still would chain thee,
  And Time his flight delay.
Ah, go not yet—each sad regret
  But chides the thought of starting:
Too soon, alas! the moments pass
  That bring the hour of parting.

Oh, why should time deceive us,
  Or joys fly with the years?
Like April smiles they leave us,
  And melt away in tears.
Companion, stay—too soon the day
  When ties of love we sever;
And still too few the friendships true
  Where hearts are linked forever.

PIO NONO.

Feb. 7, 1878.

T'was in Sinigaglia, at a shrine
An aged woman knelt, and bow'd her head;
Upon her face a sorrow half divine;
Unto her neighbors sorrowing she said,
In mournful accents, "the good Pope is dead!"

Then she recalled his gentle ways and face,
When but an humble priest his flock he fed
With words of wisdom and exceeding grace,
    And tears fell fast as tenderly
       she said
    To sobbing kindred, "the good
       Pope is dead!"

What he had done for comfort of
    the poor,
The widow and the orphan,
    and to spread
The joy of heavenly love from
    door to door,
This she remembered as, with
    reverend head
She still repeated, "the good
    Pope is dead!"

Along the bay the winter sun
    shone bright,
And o'er the crisp cool waters
    gayly sped
The lateen sails, like wings of
    life and light
While fervently with heaven
    her sad voice plead
For saintly glory for the good
    Pope dead.

Above her rose the vast Cathedral's dome;
   From niche and vault shone many a sculptured head
Of saints who toiled to build a mightier Rome
   Than Cæsar knew; unheeding then she said,
   Filled with his presence, "the good Pope is dead!"

So shall all people say, forgetting strife,
   As o'er the world the mournful tidings spread,
How well he walked the thorny ways of life
   And o'er the darkest paths the sweetness shed
   Of love and gentleness—"the good Pope is dead."

FOR HIS MERCY ENDURETH FOREVER.

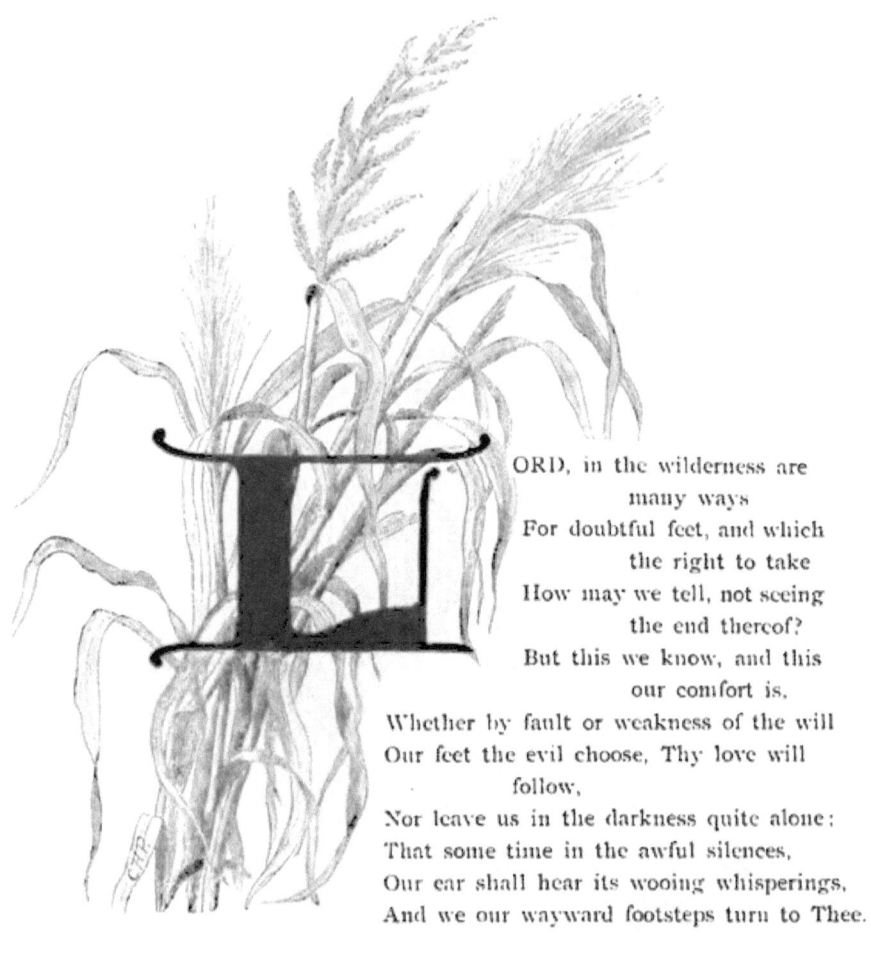

LORD, in the wilderness are
many ways
For doubtful feet, and which
the right to take
How may we tell, not seeing
the end thereof?
But this we know, and this
our comfort is,
Whether by fault or weakness of the will
Our feet the evil choose, Thy love will
follow,
Nor leave us in the darkness quite alone;
That some time in the awful silences,
Our ear shall hear its wooing whisperings,
And we our wayward footsteps turn to Thee.

www.ingramcontent.com/pod-product-compliance
Lightning Source LLC
Chambersburg PA
CBHW020829190426
43197CB00037B/739